HIS STRUGGLES

RELATIONSHIP CHALLENGES

DR. MATHEO J. SMITH JP

No part of this book may be reproduced or utilized in any form or by any means, electronic or mechanical, including photocopying, recording, or by any information storage and retrieval system, without permission in writing from the publisher.

Copyright 2024 © by Dr. Matheo J. Smith

Published by:
Ellis & Ellis Consulting Group, LLC.
www.ellisandellisconsulting.org
954-439-0760

Photography
FAUST by Nathan Faustin

CONTENTS

INTRODUCTION 4

CHAPTER 1: UNDERSTANDING GENDER DYNAMICS 6

CHAPTER 2: COMMUNICATION BARRIERS 18

CHAPTER 3: EMOTIONAL CHALLENGES 31

CHAPTER 4: FINANCIAL PRESSURES 43

CHAPTER 5: WORK-LIFE BALANCE 55

CHAPTER 6: SOCIETAL EXPECTATIONS 67

CHAPTER 7: HEALTH AND WELLBEING 80

CHAPTER 8: EDUCATIONAL DISPARITIES 92

CHAPTER 9: RELATIONSHIP DYNAMICS 105

CHAPTER 10: PARENTING PRESSURES 117

CHAPTER 11: TECHNOLOGY AND RELATIONSHIPS 129

CHAPTER 12: PERSONAL GROWTH AND DEVELOPMENT 142

CHAPTER 13: FINDING COMMON GROUND 154

INTRODUCTION

In the complex tapestry of human relationships, countless threads weave together to form the intricate patterns of connection, love, and companionship. Yet, amidst the vibrant colors of affection and understanding, there are often darker strands that signify the challenges and struggles faced by couples. 'Her Issues, His Struggles: Relationship Challenges' delves into these very threads, exploring the multifaceted dynamics that both strengthen and test the bonds between partners.

At the heart of every relationship lies a unique blend of personalities, expectations, and histories. Each partner brings their own set of experiences and emotional baggage, which can either enhance the relationship or create friction. This book seeks to unravel the common issues that women face in relationships, juxtaposed with the struggles that men encounter. It examines how societal norms, communication barriers, and personal insecurities can manifest differently for each gender, yet often lead to similar feelings of frustration and disconnect.

Through a series of insightful narratives and expert analyses, readers will gain a deeper understanding of how these challenges can be addressed and overcome. The book provides a platform for both partners to voice their concerns and perspectives, fostering empathy and mutual respect. By highlighting real-life scenarios and psychological insights, it offers practical solutions for navigating the turbulent waters of relationship conflicts.

This exploration is not merely about identifying problems but is also about recognizing the potential for growth and transformation. It encourages readers to look beyond the immediate conflicts and to appreciate the underlying love and commitment that brought them together. By understanding and addressing 'Her Issues' and 'His Struggles,' couples can forge stronger, more resilient partnerships that withstand the test of time. This book serves as a guide for those seeking to deepen their understanding of themselves and their partners, ultimately leading to more fulfilling and harmonious relationships.

Chapter 1: Understanding Gender Dynamics

Historical Context

The intricate dynamics between women's issues and men's struggles are deeply rooted in historical context, tracing back to ancient civilizations. Understanding these interactions necessitates a journey through time, examining how societal structures, gender roles, and cultural norms have shaped the experiences of both genders. In the earliest societies, gender roles were often defined by survival needs. Men typically assumed roles as hunters and protectors, while women were gatherers and caretakers. These roles were not only practical but also served as the foundation for societal organization. Over time, as societies evolved, these roles became more rigid, often to the detriment of women's autonomy and freedom. In ancient Greece and Rome, women were generally excluded from political life and were expected to adhere to domestic responsibilities. The influence of these civilizations persists, as they laid the groundwork for Western societal norms that would endure for centuries. Similarly, in many parts of Asia, Africa, and the Americas, traditional roles were enforced, often with a patriarchal structure that prioritized male authority. The Middle Ages in Europe saw the continuation of these gender norms, with women largely confined to roles within the home. However, the period also witnessed the rise of powerful female figures, such as queens and noblewomen, who navigated these constraints to exert influence. Despite these examples, the predominant narrative remained one of male dominance and female subservience. The Enlightenment era brought about significant shifts in thinking, emphasizing individual rights and equality. Yet, these ideals were slow to translate into gender equality. Women's issues began to gain more attention, leading to early feminist movements in the 19th century. This period saw the emergence of women advocating for suffrage, education, and legal rights. Meanwhile, men grappled with the challenges of industrialization and its impact on traditional roles. The 20th century marked a turning point, with two World Wars necessitating women's entry into the workforce. This shift challenged existing gender norms and laid the groundwork for the feminist movements of the 1960s and 1970s. These movements sought to dismantle systemic barriers and redefine gender roles, emphasizing equality and empowerment. As women made strides in achieving greater autonomy, men faced their own set of struggles. The changing economic landscape and evolving family dynamics required a reevaluation of masculinity and traditional male roles. The latter half of the 20th century saw a growing awareness of men's issues, including mental health, work-life balance, and societal expectations. Today, the historical context of gender dynamics continues to influence contemporary discussions. While significant progress has been made, the legacy of historical gender roles persists, manifesting in subtle and overt ways. Women continue to face issues related to representation, equality, and rights, while men navigate evolving expectations and pressures. Understanding this historical context is crucial for addressing the current challenges faced by both genders. It provides insight into the roots of these issues and highlights the necessity for continued dialogue and action to achieve a more equitable society. By examining the past, we can better understand the present and work towards a future where both women and men can thrive without the constraints of outdated norms.

Cultural Influences

The dynamics between individuals are often significantly shaped by the cultural contexts in which they exist. Culture provides a framework of norms, values, and expectations that influence behavior, communication, and perceptions of relationships. In many ways, culture acts as an invisible hand that guides interactions, often dictating what is considered acceptable or taboo within a relationship. This cultural backdrop can either facilitate harmony or become a source of conflict, depending on how well the individuals involved align with their cultural expectations or how they navigate cultural differences.

Cultural norms can dictate gender roles, influencing how men and women perceive their responsibilities within a relationship. In some cultures, traditional gender roles may be more rigid, with expectations that men should be the primary breadwinners and women should manage the domestic sphere. These roles can impact how each partner views their contributions and obligations, potentially leading to tension if there is a mismatch between cultural expectations and personal beliefs or circumstances. For example, a man who feels pressured to fulfill a traditional role as a provider may struggle if his partner also desires to pursue a career, leading to discussions about balance and fairness in responsibilities.

Communication styles are another aspect heavily influenced by cultural backgrounds. High-context cultures, which rely on implicit communication and shared understanding, might lead to misunderstandings when interacting with individuals from low-context cultures, where direct and explicit communication is the norm. Such differences can result in one partner feeling misunderstood or that their needs are not being adequately addressed. Recognizing these differences and making conscious efforts to bridge communication gaps can be crucial in maintaining a healthy relationship.

Furthermore, cultural influences extend to conflict resolution strategies. Some cultures emphasize harmony and avoidance of confrontation, advocating for indirect approaches to resolving disputes. Others might encourage direct confrontation and open discussion to address issues head-on. If partners come from different cultural backgrounds regarding conflict resolution, they may find themselves at odds over how to handle disagreements, potentially exacerbating tensions rather than alleviating them.

Cultural beliefs about love, marriage, and family also play a significant role. In some cultures, marriage is seen as a union between families rather than just individuals, which can introduce additional layers of expectations and pressures. The involvement of extended family in relationship matters can be a source of support but also a stressor if their expectations clash with the couple's own desires. Understanding and negotiating these cultural nuances requires sensitivity and a willingness to engage in open dialogue.

Moreover, cultural evolution and globalization have introduced new dynamics as individuals increasingly encounter and form relationships with those from different cultural backgrounds. This blending of cultures can enrich relationships, offering diverse perspectives and experiences. However, it can also present challenges as partners strive to integrate different cultural values and practices into their shared lives. Successfully navigating these cultural influences often involves a combination of respect, adaptability, and a commitment to understanding each other's cultural backgrounds. Ultimately, acknowledging and addressing the cultural factors at play can lead to stronger, more resilient relationships.

Psychological Perspectives

Understanding the psychological dimensions of the dynamics between women's issues and men's struggles requires a deep dive into various theories and concepts that have been developed over the years. Psychology offers a rich tapestry of perspectives that help illuminate the underlying factors contributing to these gender-related challenges. One of the foundational perspectives in psychology is the psychoanalytic view, which suggests that early childhood experiences significantly shape adult behavior and interpersonal relationships. Sigmund Freud's theories, for instance, highlight how unresolved childhood conflicts and parental influences can manifest in adult life, affecting how individuals relate to their partners and navigate personal challenges. This perspective underscores the importance of examining one's past to understand present behaviors and emotional responses.

Another critical psychological perspective is the behavioral approach, which focuses on learned behaviors and the influence of the environment on individual actions. According to behaviorists, both women's issues and men's struggles can be seen as responses to environmental stimuli, shaped by reinforcement and punishment.

This perspective suggests that understanding the patterns of reinforcement in one's life can provide insight into why certain behaviors persist and how they can be altered. For instance, a man who struggles with emotional expression may have been conditioned from a young age to believe that showing vulnerability is a sign of weakness, thus reinforcing a more stoic demeanor.

Cognitive psychology, which examines internal mental processes, provides another lens through which to view these gender-specific challenges. Cognitive theories emphasize the role of thoughts, beliefs, and perceptions in shaping behavior and emotions. Cognitive distortions, such as overgeneralization or catastrophizing, can contribute to the way individuals perceive their issues and struggles. For example, a woman dealing with self-esteem issues might view a single failure as indicative of her overall incompetence, thus exacerbating her sense of inadequacy. Cognitive-behavioral therapy (CBT), a widely used therapeutic approach, aims to address these distortions by helping individuals reframe their thinking patterns to foster healthier emotional and behavioral outcomes.

The humanistic perspective, championed by psychologists like Carl Rogers and Abraham Maslow, emphasizes personal growth and self-actualization. This approach posits that individuals have an inherent desire to achieve their fullest potential and that understanding oneself is key to overcoming personal challenges. Humanistic psychology encourages self-exploration and self-acceptance, promoting the idea that individuals can find solutions to their struggles by tapping into their inner resources and strengths.

Social psychology offers yet another valuable perspective by examining how societal norms, roles, and expectations influence individual behavior. Gender roles, in particular, play a significant role in shaping the experiences of both women and men. Social psychologists study how conformity to these roles can lead to internal conflicts and societal pressures, impacting mental health and interpersonal relationships. Understanding the social context in which these issues and struggles arise can provide insight into the broader influences that affect individual behavior and well-being.

Each of these psychological perspectives offers unique insights into the complex interplay of factors that contribute to women's issues and men's struggles. By integrating these diverse viewpoints, a more comprehensive understanding of these challenges can be achieved, paving the way for more effective interventions and support systems. The exploration of psychological theories thus becomes a crucial step in addressing and mitigating the issues and struggles faced by individuals across genders.

Current Trends

In recent years, the dynamics between genders have been evolving, driven by a myriad of social, economic, and technological factors. One of the most significant trends is the increasing recognition of gender equality and the push for women's rights in various spheres of life. This movement has brought about significant changes in workplace dynamics, family structures, and societal roles, challenging traditional norms and expectations. Women are increasingly occupying leadership positions and making their voices heard in sectors historically dominated by men. This shift is not only changing the way organizations operate but is also influencing the domestic sphere, where traditional gender roles are being redefined.

The rise of digital technology and social media platforms has amplified these changes, providing women with tools to advocate for their rights and share their experiences on a global scale. Movements like #MeToo have highlighted issues of harassment and inequality, sparking widespread conversations and leading to policy changes in many organizations. These platforms have become a space for solidarity and support, where individuals can connect, share stories, and mobilize for collective action.

On the other hand, men are facing their own set of challenges as societal expectations shift. The traditional notion of masculinity is being questioned, with increasing emphasis on emotional intelligence, vulnerability, and mental health. Men are being encouraged to express their emotions and seek help when needed, breaking away from the stereotype of stoic masculinity. This change is fostering healthier relationships and promoting a more inclusive understanding of gender roles.

Another current trend is the growing awareness and acceptance of diverse gender identities and expressions. The binary understanding of gender is increasingly being challenged, with more people identifying as non-binary, genderqueer, or genderfluid.

This shift is leading to more inclusive policies and practices in various sectors, from education to healthcare, ensuring that people of all gender identities are respected and represented. In the realm of family dynamics, there is a noticeable trend towards shared parenting responsibilities. More couples are opting for arrangements where childcare and household duties are divided more equally, allowing both partners to pursue their careers and personal interests. This trend is also reflected in the increasing number of fathers taking paternity leave and actively participating in child-rearing. Economically, the gender pay gap remains a critical issue, though progress is being made. More organizations are committing to transparency in pay practices and implementing measures to ensure equal pay for equal work. Additionally, women entrepreneurs are making strides, with more women starting businesses and leading successful ventures, contributing to economic growth and innovation.

These current trends indicate a broader cultural shift towards gender inclusivity and equality. While challenges remain, the progress made thus far highlights the potential for continued positive change. As society moves forward, it will be crucial to maintain momentum, ensuring that both women and men can navigate their issues and struggles with growth, equality, and mutual respect.

Chapter 2: Communication Barriers

Different Styles

In the realm of interpersonal dynamics, individuals often exhibit a spectrum of styles that influence how they navigate their relationships and personal challenges. These styles are not merely superficial traits but are deeply rooted in personal experiences, cultural backgrounds, and individual temperaments. Understanding these diverse styles is crucial for both personal growth and fostering harmonious relationships.

One of the most prevalent styles is the 'communicative style.' This style is characterized by an individual's ability to express thoughts and emotions openly. People who adopt this style tend to prioritize transparency and clarity in their interactions. They often seek to resolve conflicts through dialogue and value the importance of mutual understanding. However, this style can sometimes be perceived as overwhelming or intrusive by those who are less expressive.

Contrasting with the communicative approach is the 'reserved style.' Individuals who lean towards this style often prefer to process their thoughts internally before sharing them with others. They may appear distant or unapproachable at times, but this is usually a reflection of their introspective nature. They value privacy and often require time to articulate their feelings. This style can be challenging for partners or friends who crave immediate feedback or reassurance.

Another significant style is the 'problem-solving style.' People with this approach are often pragmatic and solution-oriented. They focus on addressing issues directly and efficiently, often viewing emotional discussions as secondary to finding tangible resolutions. While this style can lead to effective problem resolution, it can also overlook the emotional nuances that are crucial in many interpersonal situations.

The 'emotional style,' in contrast, places a strong emphasis on feelings and emotional connection. Individuals who exhibit this style prioritize empathy and emotional support in their interactions. They are often attuned to the emotional undercurrents in relationships and seek to nurture a deep emotional bond with others. However, this style can sometimes lead to emotional overwhelm or dependency if not balanced with practical considerations.

Cultural influences also play a vital role in shaping these styles. For instance, some cultures emphasize collectivism and community, which can foster a more collaborative and harmonious style of interaction. Others may prioritize individualism and independence, leading to styles that value self-reliance and personal autonomy. Understanding these cultural nuances is essential in appreciating the diversity of styles present in any given relationship.

Furthermore, personal experiences such as upbringing, past relationships, and life challenges significantly impact one's style. A person who has experienced trauma may develop a protective style, characterized by caution and self-preservation. Conversely, someone who has been nurtured in a supportive environment may adopt a more open and trusting style.

Recognizing and appreciating these different styles is fundamental in navigating the complexities of human relationships. It allows individuals to approach interactions with empathy and understanding, acknowledging that each person brings a unique perspective shaped by their style. By fostering an environment of acceptance and adaptability, individuals can bridge the gaps between differing styles and cultivate deeper, more meaningful connections.

Misunderstandings

In any relationship, misunderstandings are inevitable, stemming from diverse backgrounds, experiences, and communication styles. These misunderstandings often arise from assumptions and misinterpretations of intentions, leading to conflicts that can strain connections. A common source of misunderstanding is the difference in communication styles between partners. While one may prioritize verbal expression, the other might rely on non-verbal cues, creating a disconnect in conveying thoughts and emotions.

Cultural differences further complicate communication, as individuals bring unique perspectives and expectations into their interactions. For instance, what is considered a sign of respect in one culture might be perceived differently in another, leading to confusion and potential discord. These cultural nuances require a heightened awareness and sensitivity to appreciate the diversity each partner brings to the relationship.

Moreover, personal past experiences significantly influence how individuals interpret present interactions. Someone who has experienced betrayal may view a partner's innocuous actions with suspicion, creating a barrier to trust. This lens of past experiences can cloud judgment, making it challenging to see situations objectively.

Misunderstandings also frequently occur when individuals project their feelings and fears onto their partners. Insecurity about oneself can manifest as jealousy or doubt, leading to misinterpretations of a partner's behavior. This projection of insecurities can create a cycle of misunderstanding, where both parties feel misunderstood and undervalued.

Another aspect to consider is the role of language and tone in communication. Words, when spoken in haste or anger, can be misinterpreted, leaving lasting impacts on the relationship. Tone, which carries the emotional weight of words, can alter the intended meaning, leading to further confusion. Being mindful of how words are expressed is crucial in minimizing misunderstandings.

Technology, while a valuable tool for communication, also adds a layer of complexity. Text messages and emails lack the nuances of face-to-face interaction, often leading to misinterpretations. The absence of vocal tone and body language can result in messages being perceived as harsher or more indifferent than intended.

To navigate these challenges, it is essential for partners to prioritize open and honest communication. Actively listening to one another, seeking clarification, and expressing emotions transparently can help bridge the gap of misunderstanding. Practicing empathy, where each partner strives to understand the other's perspective, fosters a deeper connection and reduces the likelihood of conflicts.

Building a strong foundation of trust and patience is also vital. Trust allows partners to give each other the benefit of the doubt, reducing the tendency to assume negative intentions. Patience provides the space needed to navigate misunderstandings without escalating tensions.

Ultimately, acknowledging that misunderstandings are a natural part of any relationship can pave the way for growth. By addressing these issues thoughtfully and with compassion, partners can transform misunderstandings into opportunities for learning and strengthening their bond.

Through continuous effort and understanding, couples can overcome the struggles posed by misunderstandings, paving the way for a more harmonious and fulfilling relationship.

Conflict Resolution

In relationships, conflicts are inevitable and can arise from a multitude of sources ranging from minor misunderstandings to significant disagreements about core values. Understanding the dynamics of conflict resolution is crucial for maintaining a healthy relationship. The process involves several steps that require both parties to actively participate and engage in dialogue. The first step in resolving conflicts is acknowledging the presence of a problem. Both partners must be aware that an issue exists, which can sometimes be challenging as individuals might have different perceptions of the same situation. Acknowledgment sets the stage for open communication, which is essential for effective conflict resolution.

Open communication involves expressing feelings and thoughts honestly and respectfully. It is important for each partner to articulate their perspective without fear of retribution or dismissal. This often requires setting aside time to discuss issues without distractions. Active listening plays a crucial role in this phase. Each partner should listen to understand, rather than to respond. This means fully concentrating, understanding, and responding thoughtfully to the other person's concerns. Empathy is also critical, as it allows individuals to put themselves in their partner's shoes, fostering a deeper understanding of their feelings and viewpoints.

Once both partners have expressed their concerns, the next step involves identifying the underlying issues. Often, conflicts are symptoms of deeper problems such as unmet needs, past grievances, or differing expectations. By identifying these root causes, couples can address the core issues rather than merely treating the symptoms. This requires both partners to be introspective and honest about their needs and desires.

After identifying the core issues, brainstorming solutions together is vital. This step involves collaboratively coming up with potential solutions that are acceptable to both parties. It is important for the couple to approach this phase with an open mind and a willingness to compromise. Solutions should be realistic and consider the needs of both partners. Compromise is often necessary, and both individuals should be prepared to give and take.

Implementing the agreed-upon solutions is the next critical step. Both partners must commit to taking action and making changes that will prevent the conflict from recurring. This might involve changing certain behaviors, establishing new boundaries, or finding new ways to meet each other's needs. Commitment to change is essential for the success of the resolution process.

Finally, evaluating the effectiveness of the solutions is a crucial part of conflict resolution. This involves both partners reflecting on whether the implemented changes have improved the situation. If not, further adjustments might be necessary. Continuous communication and feedback are essential to ensure that both partners feel satisfied with the resolution.

Conflict resolution is a dynamic and ongoing process that requires patience, understanding, and mutual respect. It is not about winning or losing but about finding a path forward that strengthens the relationship. By following these steps, couples can navigate conflicts more effectively, paving the way for a healthier and more harmonious relationship.

Building Bridges

In the intricate dance of relationships, understanding and empathy play pivotal roles in bridging the divide between individual experiences. The dynamics of 'Her Issues' and 'His Struggles' often manifest in communication gaps, emotional misunderstandings, and differing expectations. This subchapter delves into the strategies and mindsets necessary for building bridges that connect these disparate worlds, fostering a more harmonious coexistence.

Effective communication forms the backbone of any strong relationship. It requires not just the articulation of thoughts and feelings but also the active listening and validation of the partner's perspective. Miscommunication often stems from preconceived notions and stereotypes, which can lead to assumptions about a partner's intentions or emotions. By cultivating a habit of open dialogue, couples can dismantle these barriers and replace them with mutual understanding.

Another critical aspect is the willingness to see beyond one's own perspective. Empathy involves stepping into another person's shoes, attempting to grasp their feelings and motivations genuinely. For 'Her Issues,' this might mean recognizing the societal pressures and personal challenges that women face, which can affect their emotional responses and behaviors. Conversely, understanding 'His Struggles' involves acknowledging the burdens of expectations placed on men, whether in terms of career success, emotional stoicism, or familial responsibilities. By appreciating these unique challenges, partners can offer more tailored support and understanding.

The concept of emotional intelligence is also central to building bridges in relationships. This involves being aware of one's emotions, as well as those of others, and managing these emotions constructively. Emotional intelligence helps partners navigate conflicts, diffuse tensions, and foster a nurturing environment. It encourages individuals to regulate their reactions, communicate their needs effectively, and respond to their partner with compassion rather than judgment.

Shared experiences and collaborative problem-solving can further solidify the bond between partners. Engaging in activities that both partners enjoy or embarking on new ventures together can create shared memories that strengthen the relationship. These experiences provide a foundation for understanding each other's likes, dislikes, and aspirations, making it easier to support each other through personal challenges. Moreover, setting clear and mutually agreed-upon goals can align partners on a common path. This could involve planning for future milestones, whether they pertain to career aspirations, family planning, or personal growth. When both partners have a clear understanding of what they are working towards, it minimizes conflicts arising from misaligned priorities or unmet expectations.

Lastly, patience and perseverance are essential virtues in the journey of building bridges. Change and understanding do not happen overnight, and setbacks are a natural part of any relationship. However, by maintaining a commitment to growth and understanding, partners can overcome obstacles and strengthen their bond over time. A relationship built on mutual respect and empathy is one where both 'Her Issues' and 'His Struggles' are acknowledged, and addressed in a way that benefits the partnership as a whole.

Chapter 3: Emotional Challenges

Recognizing Feelings

Understanding emotions is a fundamental aspect of navigating both personal and relational landscapes. Emotions serve as internal signals, providing insights into our mental and emotional states and influencing our interactions with others. Recognizing feelings involves identifying and acknowledging the emotions we experience in various situations. This process is crucial for fostering self-awareness and improving communication within relationships.

Emotions can be complex, often presenting as a combination of multiple feelings. For instance, a person may feel both anger and sadness in response to a particular event. By recognizing these emotions, individuals can better understand the underlying causes of their reactions and address them more effectively. This awareness allows for a more thoughtful response rather than an impulsive reaction, which can lead to healthier interactions and resolutions.

The ability to recognize feelings is not innate; it requires practice and reflection. Many people struggle with identifying their emotions due to societal conditioning or personal upbringing that discourages emotional expression. In some cultures, expressing emotions such as sadness or anger may be viewed as a sign of weakness, leading individuals to suppress these feelings. Over time, this suppression can result in an inability to recognize or articulate emotions, creating a barrier to effective communication and emotional health.

Developing emotional recognition skills involves several strategies. One approach is mindfulness, which encourages individuals to observe their thoughts and feelings without judgment. By practicing mindfulness, individuals can become more attuned to their emotional states and learn to recognize patterns in their emotional responses. This practice can be as simple as taking a moment each day to reflect on one's feelings and consider what might be influencing them.

Another strategy is journaling, which provides a space for individuals to explore and document their emotions. Writing about feelings can help clarify thoughts and provide insights into emotional triggers and patterns.

Journaling can also serve as a tool for tracking emotional growth over time, highlighting progress in emotional recognition and management.

Communication plays a critical role in recognizing and expressing feelings within relationships. Open dialogue allows individuals to share their emotional experiences and understand those of their partners. By discussing emotions openly, partners can foster empathy and support, strengthening their emotional connection. This process requires active listening and a willingness to validate each other's feelings, even when they differ from one's own.

Recognizing feelings also involves understanding the physiological responses associated with emotions. Physical cues such as increased heart rate, muscle tension, or changes in breathing can indicate underlying emotions. By paying attention to these signals, individuals can gain further insight into their emotional states and respond more effectively.

Ultimately, recognizing feelings is a crucial skill for personal development and relational harmony. It enables individuals to navigate their emotional landscapes with greater clarity and fosters healthier, more empathetic relationships. By cultivating this skill, individuals can enhance their emotional intelligence, leading to more fulfilling and resilient connections.

Expressing Emotions

In the intricate dance of human interaction, expressing emotions is a fundamental aspect that shapes relationships and personal well-being. Understanding how to effectively convey emotions is crucial, as it determines how individuals connect with one another and navigate the complexities of interpersonal dynamics. In the context of the challenges faced by both genders, the ability to express emotions can differ significantly, influenced by societal norms, upbringing, and personal experiences.

For many, expressing emotions is synonymous with vulnerability, a state that some might find uncomfortable or even daunting. This is particularly true in societies where traditional gender roles dictate how men and women should behave emotionally. Men, for instance, are often socialized to exhibit strength and resilience, sometimes at the expense of emotional openness. This can lead to struggles in articulating feelings, which might be perceived as a sign of weakness. The internalization of such norms can result in emotional suppression, affecting mental health and relationship satisfaction.

Conversely, women may face a different set of expectations. They are frequently encouraged to be more emotionally expressive, yet this can also be a double-edged sword. While openness is typically more socially accepted, women might encounter stereotypes that label them as overly emotional or irrational. This dichotomy can lead to a conflict where women feel pressured to modulate their emotional expressions to fit societal expectations, sometimes leading to misunderstandings and relational discord.

Effective communication of emotions requires a delicate balance and an understanding of one's emotional landscape. It involves recognizing and naming feelings, a skill that not everyone possesses naturally. Emotional literacy, the ability to identify and articulate feelings, plays a crucial role in this process. It is an acquired skill that can be developed through self-reflection and practice. For individuals struggling with emotional expression, engaging in activities such as journaling or mindfulness can help in gaining insight into their emotional states.

Moreover, creating a supportive environment where emotions are validated and respected is essential for healthy expression. This involves active listening and empathy from both parties in a relationship. When individuals feel heard and understood, they are more likely to share their emotions openly. This, in turn, strengthens the bond between them, fostering a deeper connection and mutual understanding.

Cultural influences also play a significant role in how emotions are expressed. Different cultures have varying norms regarding emotional expression, which can impact individuals' comfort levels and expectations. Being aware of these cultural nuances is important, especially in multicultural settings, to avoid misinterpretations and to promote inclusivity.

Ultimately, expressing emotions is an integral part of the human experience, influencing how individuals relate to themselves and others. By cultivating emotional awareness and communication skills, individuals can better navigate the challenges posed by societal expectations and personal struggles. This not only enhances personal well-being but also enriches relationships, paving the way for more meaningful and fulfilling connections.

Dealing with Stress

Stress is an inevitable aspect of life, impacting individuals across various spectrums, often manifesting differently in men and women. Understanding these differences is crucial in addressing the unique challenges faced by each gender. In the context of 'Her Issues, His Struggles,' exploring how stress is perceived and managed by both genders offers valuable insights into effective coping mechanisms and support systems.

For women, stress often intertwines with emotional and relational aspects of their lives. The demands of balancing work, family, and social responsibilities can lead to heightened stress levels. Women are more likely to express their stress through emotional outlets, seeking social support from friends and family. This inclination towards verbalizing stress can be beneficial, as it fosters a sense of community and shared understanding. However, it can also lead to emotional exhaustion if not managed properly. Women may benefit from structured stress management techniques like mindfulness and meditation, which promote relaxation and emotional resilience.

Men, on the other hand, tend to internalize stress, often viewing it as a challenge to be overcome independently. Societal expectations of masculinity may discourage men from openly expressing vulnerability, leading to a more stoic approach to stress. This can result in physical manifestations of stress, such as headaches or high blood pressure, if not addressed. Men might find it helpful to engage in physical activities, such as sports or exercise, which provide an outlet for stress relief and promote a sense of achievement.

While the biological responses to stress are similar in both genders, the psychological and social interpretations can vary significantly. Women's stress responses are often linked to the release of oxytocin, which enhances the desire for social bonding as a coping mechanism. In contrast, men's stress responses are more associated with the fight-or-flight reaction, prompting a more action-oriented approach.

Recognizing these differences is essential for developing effective stress management strategies. For both men and women, fostering an environment that encourages open communication about stress can lead to healthier coping mechanisms. Workplaces and communities that prioritize mental health awareness create spaces where individuals feel comfortable seeking help without fear of stigma.

Moreover, incorporating stress-reducing activities into daily routines can significantly improve overall well-being. Techniques such as time management, setting realistic goals, and prioritizing self-care are universally beneficial. Encouraging both men and women to engage in activities that promote relaxation, such as yoga or creative hobbies, can also be effective in mitigating stress.

Ultimately, the key to dealing with stress lies in understanding and respecting the diverse ways individuals experience and cope with it. By acknowledging the unique challenges faced by each gender, we can foster a more empathetic and supportive environment that empowers individuals to manage stress effectively. This holistic approach not only enhances personal well-being but also strengthens relationships and communities, creating a more resilient society.

Emotional Support

In relationships, emotional support plays a pivotal role in fostering a strong and healthy connection between partners.

It serves as a foundation that helps individuals navigate the complexities of their personal and shared experiences. Emotional support involves understanding, empathy, and a willingness to be present for each other, especially during challenging times. This form of support is not just about offering solutions but also about providing a safe space where partners can express their feelings without fear of judgment.

Effective emotional support requires active listening. It is important for partners to genuinely listen to each other, which means giving full attention and acknowledging the emotions being expressed. This can be challenging in a world filled with distractions, but making a conscious effort to focus on the other person can significantly enhance the quality of the support provided. Active listening involves not only hearing the words but also understanding the underlying emotions and context.

Empathy is another crucial component of emotional support. It involves putting oneself in the other person's shoes and trying to understand their perspective and feelings. Empathy goes beyond sympathy, which is merely feeling sorry for someone. Instead, it requires a deeper connection and an effort to comprehend the emotional experience of the partner. When partners demonstrate empathy, it helps to build trust and strengthens the emotional bond between them.

Moreover, emotional support is about being present, both physically and emotionally. This presence can manifest in various ways, such as offering a comforting hug, providing a listening ear, or simply being there in silence when words are not necessary. The act of being present reassures the partner that they are not alone in their struggles and that they have someone to lean on.

It is also important to recognize that emotional support is a two-way street. Both partners should be willing to give and receive support. It is not only about one partner constantly being the supporter while the other is the recipient. A balanced relationship involves mutual support, where both individuals feel valued and understood. This reciprocity helps to maintain a healthy dynamic and prevents one partner from feeling overwhelmed or neglected.

Communication is key in providing effective emotional support. Partners should openly discuss their needs and boundaries related to emotional support. Understanding each other's preferences and limits can prevent misunderstandings and ensure that both parties feel comfortable and respected. This open dialogue can lead to a more tailored and effective support system within the relationship.

Challenges may arise when partners have different approaches to giving and receiving emotional support. Some individuals may prefer verbal encouragement, while others might appreciate physical affection or practical help. Recognizing and respecting these differences is essential in providing meaningful support. Flexibility and adaptability in one's approach can help bridge these differences and enhance the emotional connection.

Ultimately, emotional support is about nurturing the emotional well-being of both partners. It requires a commitment to understanding, empathy, and presence, which collectively contribute to a deeper and more resilient relationship. By prioritizing emotional support, couples can better navigate the ups and downs of life together, fostering a partnership built on trust, compassion, and mutual respect.

Chapter 4: Financial Pressures

Income Inequality

Income inequality is a pervasive issue that significantly impacts both individuals and societies at large. It refers to the unequal distribution of income and wealth across various participants in an economy. This disparity can manifest in various forms, such as differences in wages, salaries, and overall wealth accumulation among different groups, often categorized by demographics like gender, race, and geographic location. In exploring the dynamics of income inequality, it is crucial to understand its origins and the factors that perpetuate it.

One of the primary drivers of income inequality is the disparity in educational opportunities. Education is a critical determinant of economic success, and access to quality education often varies significantly across different segments of the population. Individuals from affluent backgrounds typically have access to better educational resources, which increases their chances of attaining higher-paying jobs. Conversely, those from less privileged backgrounds may face numerous barriers, limiting their economic prospects and perpetuating the cycle of poverty.

Another significant factor contributing to income inequality is the labor market structure. The labor market is often segmented, with high-paying jobs concentrated in certain industries and requiring specific skill sets. Technological advancements have further exacerbated this divide, as they have created a demand for highly skilled workers while reducing the need for low-skilled labor. This shift has led to a widening gap between those who can command high wages due to their specialized skills and those who cannot.

Furthermore, income inequality is influenced by government policies and taxation systems. Tax policies that favor the wealthy, such as lower tax rates on capital gains compared to income tax rates on wages, tend to exacerbate income inequality. Additionally, insufficient social welfare systems and minimum wage laws can fail to provide adequate support for low-income individuals, leaving them at a disadvantage.

The impact of income inequality extends beyond economic dimensions, affecting social cohesion and political stability. High levels of income inequality can lead to social unrest, as individuals who feel marginalized may become disillusioned with the socio-economic system. This discontent can manifest in various forms, from increased crime rates to political polarization, as people seek to address the disparities through different means.

Gender inequality also plays a crucial role in income disparity. Women, on average, earn less than men for similar work, a phenomenon known as the gender pay gap. This gap is often attributed to various factors, including discrimination, differences in industry and occupation, and the disproportionate share of unpaid care work that women undertake. Addressing gender-based income inequality requires both policy interventions and societal shifts in attitudes towards gender roles.

Addressing income inequality necessitates a multi-faceted approach that involves reforming educational systems to ensure equal access for all, restructuring labor markets to provide opportunities for skill development, and implementing fair taxation and social welfare policies. By tackling these root causes, societies can work towards reducing income inequality, thereby fostering a more equitable and inclusive economic environment.

Budgeting and Planning

Navigating the complexities of financial management can be one of the most challenging aspects of any relationship, often requiring a delicate balance of priorities, needs, and desires. In the context of a partnership, budgeting and planning are not merely about numbers and spreadsheets; they are about understanding each partner's financial habits, goals, and values. These elements form the foundation of a stable financial future and contribute significantly to the overall health of the relationship.

Effective budgeting begins with open communication. It is essential for partners to discuss their financial history, including any debts, savings, and spending habits. This transparency helps to avoid misunderstandings and fosters trust. Once each partner's financial situation is clear, it becomes easier to set joint financial goals. Whether it's saving for a house, planning for a child's education, or preparing for retirement, having clear objectives can guide the budgeting process.

Creating a budget involves tracking income and expenses. Couples should consider all sources of income, including salaries, bonuses, and any other financial contributions.

Expenses should be categorized into fixed and variable costs. Fixed costs, such as rent or mortgage payments, utilities, and insurance, remain constant each month, while variable costs, like groceries, dining out, and entertainment, can fluctuate. By distinguishing between these categories, couples can identify areas where they might need to cut back or adjust their spending.

Once a budget is established, it is crucial to regularly review and adjust it as necessary. Life is unpredictable, and financial situations can change due to various factors such as job loss, medical emergencies, or market fluctuations. Regular check-ins allow couples to adapt their plans to meet current needs and to stay on track with their long-term goals. These reviews should be seen as opportunities to reassess priorities and ensure that both partners are aligned in their financial journey.

Planning for the future involves setting aside funds for emergencies and long-term investments. An emergency fund is a critical component of financial planning, providing a buffer against unexpected expenses. Typically, it is recommended to save three to six months' worth of living expenses. In addition to an emergency fund, couples should consider long-term investments such as retirement accounts, stocks, or real estate. These investments require careful planning and often consultation with financial advisors to maximize returns and ensure financial security.

Moreover, budgeting and planning should also incorporate an element of flexibility and personal enjoyment. Setting aside a portion of the budget for personal hobbies, date nights, or vacations can help maintain a healthy balance between financial responsibility and quality of life. It is important for each partner to feel that their individual needs and desires are acknowledged and valued.

Ultimately, successful budgeting and planning require cooperation, compromise, and a shared vision for the future. By working together to manage their finances, couples can not only achieve their financial goals but also strengthen their relationship. The process of budgeting and planning becomes a collaborative effort that reflects the partnership's collective aspirations and values, paving the way for a harmonious and prosperous future together.

Debt Management

Managing debt is an essential aspect of financial well-being, and it requires a strategic approach to ensure that it does not become overwhelming. In the context of relationships, debt management can become even more complex, as it involves not just individual financial responsibilities but also shared financial goals and obligations. Effective debt management begins with a clear understanding of the nature and extent of the debt. This involves taking stock of all outstanding debts, including credit card balances, loans, and any other financial obligations. By doing so, individuals and couples can develop a comprehensive view of their financial situation, which is crucial for devising a realistic and effective debt repayment plan.

Communication plays a pivotal role in debt management within relationships. It is important for partners to openly discuss their financial situations, including the debts they have incurred and their plans for repayment. This openness fosters trust and ensures that both parties are on the same page regarding their financial goals. Without honest communication, misunderstandings may arise, potentially leading to conflicts that can strain the relationship.

Once the debt has been clearly identified and communication established, the next step is to prioritize debts. Not all debts are created equal, and some may carry higher interest rates or more severe consequences for missed payments. By prioritizing debts, individuals and couples can focus on paying off those that are most burdensome or carry the highest interest rates first. This approach not only helps in reducing the overall debt burden more quickly but also minimizes the amount of interest paid over time.

Budgeting is another critical component of effective debt management. Creating a realistic budget that accounts for all income and expenses allows individuals and couples to allocate funds specifically for debt repayment. A well-planned budget helps in identifying areas where expenses can be reduced or cut altogether, freeing up more resources to pay down debt. It is important that the budget is adhered to strictly to ensure that debt repayment remains on track.

Additionally, exploring options for debt consolidation or refinancing can be beneficial. Consolidating multiple debts into a single loan with a lower interest rate can simplify payments and reduce the overall interest burden. Similarly, refinancing high-interest loans with more favorable terms can make debt repayment more manageable. However, these options should be considered carefully, taking into account any fees or potential risks involved.

Seeking professional financial advice can also be advantageous, especially for those who feel overwhelmed by their debt situation. Financial advisors can provide valuable insights and strategies tailored to individual circumstances, helping to navigate the complexities of debt management effectively.

Ultimately, successful debt management requires a combination of careful planning, open communication, and disciplined execution. By taking proactive steps and working together, individuals and couples can overcome the challenges posed by debt, paving the way for a more secure financial future. This not only alleviates financial stress but also strengthens the foundation of the relationship, allowing both partners to focus on their shared aspirations and dreams.

Future Security

As we navigate the complexities of modern relationships, the concept of future security emerges as a pivotal concern for both partners. This subchapter delves into the various dimensions of future security, examining how individuals perceive and plan for stability in their personal and shared lives. Future security encompasses not only financial stability but also emotional and relational assurances that partners seek to cultivate together. Understanding these aspects can mitigate anxieties and foster a more harmonious partnership.

Financial security often stands at the forefront of future planning in relationships. Partners frequently discuss and negotiate financial goals, such as saving for a home, planning for retirement, or managing current expenses. These discussions require openness and honesty about each partner's financial situation, spending habits, and long-term aspirations. Financial security is not merely about accumulating wealth but also about ensuring that both partners feel comfortable and supported in their financial decisions and obligations.

Emotional security is another critical component of future security. It involves creating a supportive environment where both partners feel valued, understood, and cared for. Emotional security is built through consistent communication, empathy, and trust. Partners need to feel that they can rely on each other in times of need and that their emotional well-being is a shared priority. This sense of security can be nurtured through regular check-ins, active listening, and validating each other's feelings and experiences.

In addition to financial and emotional aspects, relational security plays a significant role in the future stability of a partnership. Relational security involves the confidence that both partners are committed to the relationship and are willing to work through challenges together. This can be reinforced by setting mutual goals, celebrating achievements, and maintaining a strong connection through shared interests and activities. Relational security is about knowing that the partnership is a safe space where both individuals can grow and evolve together.

The pursuit of future security also involves addressing potential uncertainties and planning for unforeseen circumstances. This might include discussing topics such as health care, life insurance, and estate planning. These conversations, while often difficult, are essential for ensuring that both partners are prepared for life's unpredictabilities. Proactively addressing these issues can alleviate anxiety and provide a sense of control over future outcomes.

Moreover, future security is not a static goal but a dynamic process that evolves with the relationship. As partners grow and change, their needs and priorities may shift, necessitating ongoing dialogue and adaptation. Flexibility and resilience are key to maintaining future security, as they allow partners to navigate life's inevitable changes and challenges together.

Ultimately, future security in a relationship is about creating a foundation of trust, understanding, and mutual support. It requires both partners to actively engage in planning and communication, ensuring that their shared vision for the future aligns with their individual aspirations. By addressing the multiple facets of future security, partners can build a relationship that is not only enduring but also enriching for both individuals involved.

Chapter 5: Work-Life Balance

Career Demands

In the modern world, career demands have become an integral part of our lives, shaping not only our financial stability but also our personal identities and relationships. The pursuit of professional success often requires individuals to navigate a complex landscape of expectations, responsibilities, and pressures. This subchapter delves into the multifaceted nature of career demands, examining how they influence both personal and interpersonal dynamics.

At the core of career demands lies the expectation to perform and excel in one's chosen field. This expectation is driven by various factors, including organizational goals, industry standards, and individual aspirations. The pressure to meet these expectations can lead to long work hours, high stress levels, and a constant need for self-improvement. As individuals strive to achieve their career objectives, they often face the challenge of balancing work commitments with personal life, leading to potential conflicts and sacrifices.

Moreover, career demands are not uniform and can vary significantly across different professions and industries. For instance, high-pressure environments such as finance, healthcare, and technology often require employees to be on call beyond regular working hours, impacting their ability to disconnect from work-related stress. In contrast, other fields may offer more predictable schedules but come with their own set of demands, such as maintaining creativity and innovation.

The rapid pace of technological advancement further complicates the landscape of career demands. Professionals are increasingly expected to stay updated with the latest tools and trends, necessitating continuous learning and adaptation. This requirement for lifelong learning can be both an opportunity and a burden, as it demands time and effort that could otherwise be spent on leisure or family.

Interpersonal relationships are also significantly affected by career demands. The time and energy devoted to meeting professional expectations can strain relationships with family and friends. Partners may feel neglected, and social interactions can become limited, leading to feelings of isolation. Additionally, the competitive nature of many industries can foster environments where collaboration and teamwork are overshadowed by individual ambition, potentially hindering workplace relationships.

Gender dynamics also play a crucial role in shaping career demands. Societal expectations and stereotypes often influence how men and women perceive and handle professional pressures. Women, in particular, may face unique challenges, such as balancing career aspirations with traditional caregiving roles, which can lead to added stress and the need to navigate career breaks or part-time work. Conversely, men may experience pressure to prioritize career success over personal well-being, reinforcing traditional notions of masculinity.

Ultimately, understanding the impact of career demands involves recognizing the diverse factors that contribute to professional pressure. By acknowledging these complexities, individuals can better navigate their careers while striving for a harmonious balance between work and personal life. Organizations can also play a role by fostering supportive environments that prioritize employee well-being, offering flexible work arrangements, and encouraging open dialogue about the challenges of meeting career demands. As we continue to explore the interplay between professional and personal lives, it becomes increasingly important to address the evolving nature of career demands and their influence on our daily existence.

Family Responsibilities

Family responsibilities often serve as a pivotal aspect in the dynamics between partners, influencing both their individual and collective experiences. In many relationships, the distribution of family duties can become a source of tension, especially when expectations are misaligned or uncommunicated. Understanding how these responsibilities are perceived and managed is crucial for fostering harmony and mutual respect.

Traditionally, societal norms have often dictated specific roles for men and women within the family unit. Historically, women were expected to take on the majority of domestic duties, including child-rearing and household management, while men were typically seen as the primary breadwinners. These gender-based roles, however, have evolved significantly over time. In contemporary settings, there is a growing expectation for a more equitable sharing of family responsibilities, yet the transition is not always seamless.

The shift towards shared responsibilities can present challenges, particularly when individuals have been raised with traditional viewpoints that influence their expectations. For instance, a man who was brought up in a household where his father was the sole provider may subconsciously expect to fulfill a similar role. Conversely, a woman who witnessed her mother handling all domestic chores might feel compelled to replicate that model, even if her circumstances differ. These ingrained perceptions can lead to misunderstandings and frustration within a partnership.

Effective communication is paramount in addressing and managing family responsibilities. Couples who engage in open dialogues about their expectations and capabilities often find it easier to navigate the complexities of shared duties. Discussions should encompass not only the division of labor but also considerations of each partner's strengths, weaknesses, and preferences. For example, one partner might excel at financial planning while the other is more adept at organizing family schedules. Recognizing and leveraging these individual skills can lead to a more efficient and harmonious household.

Moreover, the influence of external factors such as employment demands, financial constraints, and cultural expectations cannot be overlooked. Job-related pressures can significantly impact the time and energy available for family responsibilities, necessitating adjustments and compromises. Financial limitations might require both partners to work outside the home, thus necessitating a more balanced approach to domestic tasks.

Cultural expectations also play a role in shaping how family responsibilities are perceived and allocated. In some cultures, extended family members are heavily involved in daily household activities, providing support and alleviating some of the burdens from the immediate family. In contrast, other cultures emphasize nuclear family independence, which can place more pressure on the couple to manage all responsibilities on their own.

Ultimately, the goal is to create a partnership where both individuals feel valued and supported. This requires a willingness to adapt and renegotiate roles as circumstances change. Flexibility and empathy are essential components in this process, as they allow partners to accommodate each other's evolving needs and challenges. By fostering an environment of cooperation and understanding, couples can transform family responsibilities from a source of contention into an opportunity for growth and connection.

Self-Care

In the contemporary landscape where life's pace is relentless and demands are perpetual, self-care emerges not merely as a luxury but an essential component of maintaining mental, emotional, and physical well-being. The concept of self-care, though often relegated to the realms of pampering and relaxation, encompasses a broader spectrum of practices that are vital for sustaining overall health. Within the dynamics of relationships, particularly where partners may face distinct challenges, self-care becomes paramount in navigating personal and shared struggles effectively.

Self-care is fundamentally about ensuring that one's own needs are met so that individuals can function optimally in various roles, whether as partners, parents, or professionals. In the context of relationships, it is crucial for both individuals to recognize the importance of self-care to prevent burnout and resentment. When each partner prioritizes their well-being, they are better equipped to support one another, fostering a healthier and more resilient relationship.

For women, societal expectations often dictate a nurturing role, which can lead to neglecting personal needs. It is vital for women to carve out time for activities that replenish their energy and spirit. This might include engaging in hobbies, physical exercise, meditation, or simply setting aside time for solitude. Such practices not only enhance personal well-being but also contribute to a more balanced and harmonious partnership. As women address their issues through self-care, they cultivate the strength and clarity needed to support their partners who may be grappling with their own struggles.

Men, on the other hand, may face societal pressures to embody stoicism and self-reliance, which can hinder their engagement in self-care practices. Encouraging men to embrace self-care involves challenging these stereotypes and understanding that taking time for oneself is not indicative of weakness, but rather a demonstration of self-awareness and responsibility. Activities that promote relaxation and personal growth, such as exercising, pursuing interests, or engaging in social activities, can significantly alleviate stress and improve overall well-being.

Furthermore, self-care is not solely an individual pursuit; it can also be a shared endeavor that strengthens the bond between partners. Couples can engage in self-care activities together, such as taking walks, cooking meals, or attending workshops that promote mutual interests. These shared experiences not only enhance the connection between partners but also provide opportunities to communicate and support each other's personal growth.

Ultimately, integrating self-care into daily routines requires dedication and intentionality. It involves setting boundaries, prioritizing tasks, and sometimes, making difficult decisions to ensure that personal health is not compromised. By acknowledging the importance of self-care, individuals within relationships can navigate their unique challenges more effectively, leading to healthier interactions and a more fulfilling partnership. Embracing self-care as a fundamental aspect of life allows both partners to thrive individually and collectively, offering the resilience needed to face life's inevitable challenges together.

Prioritizing Time

In the complex tapestry of relationships, time often emerges as both a precious commodity and a source of contention. Understanding how to prioritize time effectively can be a significant factor in addressing the issues faced by women and the struggles encountered by men within the dynamics of their interactions. The concept of time management is not merely about scheduling; it involves recognizing the value of time in nurturing relationships and balancing personal and shared responsibilities.

One critical aspect of prioritizing time is recognizing the different ways in which individuals perceive and value time. Women and men may have divergent approaches to time management, influenced by societal expectations, personal goals, and familial responsibilities. For women, there is often an expectation to juggle multiple roles simultaneously, which can lead to feelings of being overwhelmed. Men, on the other hand, might struggle with societal pressures to prioritize career advancement, sometimes at the expense of personal relationships. Understanding these differing perspectives is essential for fostering empathy and cooperation.

Effective time prioritization requires open communication between partners. Establishing a dialogue about how time is allocated can help align expectations and reduce conflicts. Couples should discuss their individual and collective goals, identifying areas where time might be reallocated to better serve both parties. This can include setting aside regular intervals for meaningful interactions, ensuring that both partners feel valued and heard.

Another aspect to consider is the impact of technology on time management within relationships. In an age where digital distractions are ubiquitous, it is easy for individuals to become disconnected from their partners. Establishing boundaries around technology use can help ensure that time spent together is genuinely engaging and fulfilling. Partners might agree to designate tech-free zones or times, allowing for uninterrupted communication and connection.

Time prioritization also involves making conscious decisions about commitments outside the relationship. Understanding the importance of saying no to certain social or professional obligations can free up time for more meaningful engagements with one's partner. This requires a mutual understanding of what commitments are truly essential and which can be adjusted or declined. By doing so, couples can create a balance that respects both individual pursuits and shared experiences.

Additionally, self-care plays a crucial role in effective time prioritization. Ensuring that each partner has time for personal growth and relaxation can enhance overall relationship satisfaction. When individuals feel fulfilled and less stressed, they are better equipped to contribute positively to the relationship. Encouraging each other to pursue hobbies, exercise, or simply take time for rest can strengthen the partnership by promoting well-being.

Cultural and familial influences can also affect how time is prioritized. It is important for partners to acknowledge these influences and discuss how they impact their relationship. By recognizing and addressing these external pressures, couples can work together to create a time management strategy that honors their unique dynamic.

Ultimately, the way time is prioritized within a relationship can significantly influence its success and longevity. By understanding differing perspectives, communicating openly, setting boundaries, and valuing self-care, partners can navigate the challenges of time management together. This collaborative approach not only addresses individual issues and struggles but also strengthens the bond between them, fostering a more harmonious and fulfilling relationship.

Chapter 6: Societal Expectations

Gender Roles

Gender roles have been a fundamental aspect of societal structures throughout history, shaping the behaviors and expectations of individuals based on their sex. These roles are deeply ingrained, influencing various facets of life including family dynamics, career choices, and personal relationships. Traditionally, gender roles have been binary, with distinct expectations for men and women. Men have often been associated with traits such as strength, assertiveness, and dominance, while women have been linked to nurturing, empathy, and submissiveness. These stereotypes have historically dictated the division of labor both in the household and the workplace, with men typically assuming the role of the breadwinner and women taking on domestic responsibilities.

In many cultures, these traditional roles have been reinforced through socialization, where individuals learn and internalize societal norms from a young age. Family, education, and media play significant roles in perpetuating these expectations, often rewarding conformity and discouraging deviation. Boys are often encouraged to engage in activities that emphasize competitiveness and leadership, while girls are directed towards nurturing and cooperative roles. This early socialization can limit personal growth and contribute to a rigid understanding of gender identity.

However, the modern era has seen a gradual shift in these perceptions, driven by social, economic, and political changes. The feminist movements of the 20th and 21st centuries have been instrumental in challenging and redefining traditional gender roles. Advocates have highlighted the limitations and inequalities inherent in these roles, calling for a more equitable distribution of responsibilities and opportunities. As a result, there has been an increasing acceptance of non-traditional roles, with more women entering the workforce and men taking on more caregiving duties.

Despite these advancements, rigid gender roles still persist in many areas, leading to significant challenges for both men and women. Women often face the 'double burden' of balancing professional careers with domestic responsibilities, which can hinder their career advancement and contribute to stress and burnout. Men, on the other hand, may struggle with the pressure to conform to traditional masculine ideals, which can limit their emotional expression and lead to mental health issues.

The concept of gender roles is further complicated by the recognition of non-binary and transgender identities, which challenge the binary framework traditionally used to understand gender. These identities underscore the importance of viewing gender as a spectrum rather than a fixed binary, allowing for a more inclusive understanding of individual experiences.

Ultimately, the reevaluation of gender roles is crucial for fostering a society that values equality and diversity. By questioning and redefining these roles, individuals can move towards a more balanced and fulfilling existence, free from the constraints of outdated stereotypes. This shift requires a collective effort to promote inclusivity, respect, and understanding across all levels of society, paving the way for future generations to thrive in an environment that embraces diversity in all its forms.

Media Influence

The pervasive reach of media in contemporary society has a profound impact on both individual perceptions and collective social norms. Media, in its various forms—television, social media, print, and digital platforms—serves as a powerful tool that shapes how individuals view themselves and others. This influence is particularly significant when examining gender roles and expectations, which are often perpetuated and reinforced through media representations.

From a young age, individuals are exposed to a myriad of media messages that communicate specific ideals regarding masculinity and femininity. These messages often dictate what is considered acceptable behavior, appearance, and roles for each gender. For women, media frequently emphasizes beauty, thinness, and a nurturing demeanor, while men are often portrayed as strong, assertive, and emotionally stoic. These stereotypical portrayals contribute to a narrow understanding of gender roles, limiting the potential for diverse expressions of identity.

The impact of these media-driven stereotypes extends beyond individual identity formation to influence societal expectations and interactions. For instance, the portrayal of women in subordinate roles can lead to the normalization of gender inequality in workplaces and social settings. Similarly, the depiction of men as dominant figures can perpetuate unhealthy power dynamics in relationships and discourage emotional vulnerability. These media narratives not only affect how individuals perceive themselves but also how they are perceived by others, affecting interpersonal relationships and societal structures.

Moreover, the advent of social media has intensified the influence of media on gender perceptions. Platforms like Instagram, TikTok, and Facebook provide a space where individuals constantly compare themselves to idealized versions of others. The curated nature of social media content often leads to unrealistic standards of beauty and success, exacerbating issues of self-esteem and body image for both men and women. The pressure to conform to these standards can lead to mental health challenges, including anxiety and depression, as individuals struggle to meet these unattainable ideals.

Despite these challenges, media also holds the potential to challenge and redefine traditional gender norms. Increasingly, there are representations in media that celebrate diversity and promote inclusivity. These narratives provide alternative role models and encourage a broader understanding of gender identity and expression. For example, television shows and films that feature strong female leads or emotionally expressive male characters challenge conventional stereotypes and offer more nuanced portrayals of gender.

It is essential for consumers to engage critically with media content, recognizing the underlying messages and questioning the stereotypes that are often presented. By fostering media literacy, individuals can develop a more informed perspective, allowing them to resist the pressure to conform to limiting gender norms. Additionally, content creators and media professionals have a responsibility to produce diverse and equitable representations that reflect the complexity of human experiences.

As society continues to evolve, the role of media in shaping gender perceptions will remain significant. By acknowledging and addressing the influence of media, there is an opportunity to create a more inclusive and equitable environment that respects and celebrates diversity in all its forms. This requires a collective effort from individuals, media creators, and policymakers to ensure that media serves as a force for positive change, rather than a perpetuator of outdated stereotypes.

Peer Pressure

Navigating the complex landscape of peer pressure is a significant challenge faced by individuals today, particularly during adolescence and young adulthood. This phenomenon occurs when individuals feel compelled to conform to the expectations, behaviors, or attitudes of their social group. The influence of peers can manifest in various forms, ranging from subtle suggestions to overt demands, and can have both positive and negative impacts on an individual's decisions and actions.

Peer pressure is often associated with negative outcomes, such as engaging in risky behaviors, including substance abuse, academic dishonesty, or delinquency. These actions are frequently driven by the desire to fit in or gain acceptance within a particular group. The fear of rejection, social isolation, or being perceived as different can be powerful motivators that lead individuals to compromise their values or judgments.

However, peer pressure is not inherently detrimental. It can also serve as a catalyst for positive change and personal growth. For example, peers can encourage each other to strive for academic excellence, participate in community service, or adopt healthier lifestyles. In such cases, peer influence can reinforce constructive habits and foster a supportive environment that promotes mutual encouragement and achievement.

The impact of peer pressure varies depending on several factors, including the individual's age, personality, level of self-esteem, and the nature of the peer group. Adolescents, who are in a critical developmental stage, are particularly susceptible to peer influence as they seek to establish their identity and sense of belonging. Those with low self-esteem or a strong desire for acceptance may be more vulnerable to negative peer pressure, while individuals with a robust sense of self and clear personal values may be better equipped to resist undesirable influences.

Understanding the dynamics of peer pressure involves recognizing the role of social networks and the interplay between individual agency and group dynamics. The pressure to conform can be exacerbated by social media platforms, where the visibility of peer behaviors and the quest for social validation are amplified. Online interactions can intensify feelings of inadequacy or exclusion, making individuals more prone to succumbing to peer influence.

To mitigate the adverse effects of peer pressure, it is crucial for individuals to develop critical thinking skills and self-awareness. Encouraging open communication about peer influence can empower individuals to make informed decisions and resist negative pressures. Building a strong support system that includes family, friends, and mentors can provide guidance and reassurance, helping individuals navigate challenging social situations.

Educational programs that focus on social and emotional learning can also play a vital role in equipping individuals with the tools needed to handle peer pressure effectively. These programs can foster resilience, enhance self-confidence, and promote assertiveness, enabling individuals to assert their values and make choices that align with their authentic selves.

In addressing peer pressure, it is essential to acknowledge both its potential risks and benefits. By fostering environments that encourage positive peer interactions and supporting individuals in developing a strong sense of self, society can help mitigate the negative effects of peer pressure while harnessing its potential to inspire and motivate.

Breaking Stereotypes

In a world where traditional gender roles have long dictated the actions and expectations of individuals, breaking stereotypes becomes a crucial endeavor. Stereotypes are simplistic generalizations about groups that can lead to misunderstandings and perpetuate harmful biases. These stereotypes, especially those related to gender, often hinder personal growth and societal progress by confining individuals to predefined roles. Men and women, alike, face the pressures of conforming to these roles, which can lead to struggles in both personal and professional spheres.

For women, the stereotype of being overly emotional or less competent in leadership positions often creates barriers to career advancement. Despite significant progress in gender equality, women still encounter the glass ceiling effect in many industries. The notion that women are more suited for nurturing roles, such as caregiving, limits their opportunities in roles perceived as requiring assertiveness and authority. This stereotype not only affects women's career trajectories but also influences their self-perception and confidence levels.

Conversely, men grapple with the stereotype of being the stoic provider, expected to suppress emotions and maintain a facade of strength. This societal expectation can lead to mental health issues, as men may feel discouraged from seeking help or expressing vulnerability. The pressure to conform to these ideals often results in a lack of emotional literacy, further perpetuating the cycle of silence and emotional suppression. Moreover, men who choose to pursue careers traditionally associated with women, such as nursing or teaching, may face stigmatization and discrimination.

Breaking these stereotypes involves challenging the normative beliefs that dictate what men and women should or should not do. Education plays a pivotal role in this process, as it helps to dismantle myths and promote understanding of individual capabilities beyond gender. Encouraging diverse representation in media and leadership positions also aids in normalizing the idea that competence and talent are not gender-specific.

Furthermore, creating spaces for open dialogue about gender expectations can foster an environment where individuals feel empowered to express their true selves. Initiatives that promote gender inclusivity in the workplace, such as flexible work arrangements and parental leave policies for all genders, contribute to breaking down these barriers. Such policies not only benefit individuals but also enhance organizational productivity and morale by valuing diverse contributions.

On a personal level, individuals can contribute to breaking stereotypes by questioning their own biases and supporting others in their pursuit of non-traditional roles. Encouragement and mentorship can play significant roles in helping others navigate the challenges of stepping outside societal norms. By acknowledging and celebrating the unique strengths and perspectives each person brings, society can move towards a more inclusive and equitable future.

Ultimately, the journey to break stereotypes is ongoing and requires collective effort from all sectors of society. By addressing the root causes and challenging the status quo, it is possible to create a world where individuals are not limited by their gender but are free to pursue their aspirations without fear of judgment or discrimination. This shift not only benefits individuals but enriches society as a whole, paving the way for a more harmonious and understanding world.

Chapter 7: Health and Wellbeing

Physical Health

The intersection of physical health and personal relationships is a multifaceted area that requires careful consideration and understanding. Physical health affects not only an individual's well-being but also the dynamics within their relationships. When discussing the physical health of individuals, especially within the context of a partnership, it's essential to recognize how it influences both partners in different ways.

Physical health encompasses a wide range of factors, including diet, exercise, sleep, and overall bodily function. For women, physical health can be closely linked to issues such as hormonal changes, reproductive health, and conditions that disproportionately affect them, like osteoporosis or certain autoimmune disorders. These health issues can sometimes lead to feelings of vulnerability or anxiety, impacting how they interact with their partners. Men, on the other hand, might face issues such as cardiovascular health, prostate health, and other gender-specific conditions that can affect their physical performance and self-esteem.

Moreover, physical health is not static; it evolves with age and lifestyle choices. Poor physical health can lead to decreased energy levels, chronic pain, or other complications that might limit one's ability to engage fully in a relationship. For instance, a partner struggling with obesity might experience low self-esteem, which can affect intimacy and communication. Similarly, chronic illnesses can place additional stress on a relationship, requiring the couple to navigate healthcare needs, emotional support, and sometimes financial burdens together.

The role of physical health in relationships is also evident in how partners support each other's health goals. Encouragement in adopting healthier lifestyles, such as engaging in regular exercise or cooking nutritious meals together, can strengthen bonds. Conversely, when one partner is unsupportive or dismissive of the other's health concerns, it can lead to tension and misunderstandings.

Communication about physical health is vital. Open discussions about health concerns, symptoms, or lifestyle changes can prevent misunderstandings and promote empathy. Partners who communicate effectively are more likely to support each other through health challenges, fostering a more resilient relationship. This communication should be approached with sensitivity and respect, acknowledging the personal nature of health issues.

The impact of physical health on relationships is further compounded by societal expectations and gender roles. Traditional gender roles might influence how individuals perceive their health and seek care. For example, men might feel pressured to downplay health issues due to societal norms that equate masculinity with toughness, potentially delaying necessary medical intervention. Women might prioritize family responsibilities over their own health, leading to neglect of personal health needs.

Healthcare professionals can play a crucial role in addressing the intersection of physical health and relationships. By providing education and resources tailored to couples, they can help partners navigate health challenges together. Encouraging joint participation in health-related activities and fostering an understanding of each other's health needs can promote a healthier relationship dynamic.

In essence, physical health is a significant component of personal relationships, influencing how partners interact, support each other, and navigate life's challenges. Recognizing and addressing the unique health needs of each partner can enhance relationship satisfaction and longevity.

Mental Health

The intricate dance between mental health and relationships is a vital aspect of understanding the dynamics within partnerships. Mental health issues can manifest in numerous ways, affecting both individuals and the couple as a whole. Recognizing the signs and implications of mental health challenges is crucial for fostering a supportive and nurturing environment.

Mental health encompasses a broad spectrum of conditions, ranging from anxiety and depression to more severe disorders like bipolar disorder and schizophrenia. Each of these conditions brings its own set of challenges, not only for the individual experiencing them but also for their partner. The stigma surrounding mental health often makes it difficult for individuals to seek help or discuss their struggles openly, which can lead to misunderstandings and strain in relationships.

Communication is a cornerstone in managing mental health within relationships. Open and honest discussions about feelings, triggers, and coping mechanisms can help partners understand each other better. It is important for both parties to feel safe in expressing their thoughts and emotions without fear of judgment or dismissal. This level of transparency can foster empathy and patience, which are essential when navigating the complexities of mental health.

Partners can play a supportive role by educating themselves about the specific mental health issues their significant other may be facing. Understanding the symptoms and treatment options can empower them to provide the necessary support. This might include accompanying their partner to therapy sessions, helping them adhere to medication regimens, or simply being a source of comfort during difficult times.

However, it is also crucial for partners to recognize their own boundaries and limitations. Supporting someone with mental health issues can be emotionally taxing, and it is essential for both individuals to maintain their well-being.

Self-care and seeking support from friends, family, or mental health professionals can help partners manage the emotional weight of their loved one's struggles.

Mental health issues can also impact the way individuals perceive themselves and their relationships. Low self-esteem, feelings of worthlessness, or a lack of motivation can lead to withdrawal and isolation. It is crucial for partners to acknowledge these feelings and work together to address them. Encouraging positive self-talk, engaging in activities that boost self-esteem, and setting achievable goals can help individuals regain a sense of purpose and connection.

In some cases, couples may benefit from joint therapy sessions, where they can explore the impact of mental health on their relationship in a structured setting. A therapist can provide guidance and strategies to improve communication, resolve conflicts, and strengthen the bond between partners. This collaborative approach can be particularly beneficial in breaking down barriers and fostering a deeper understanding of each other's experiences.

Ultimately, addressing mental health within relationships requires a commitment to compassion, patience, and continuous learning. By prioritizing mental well-being, couples can navigate their struggles more effectively and build a resilient partnership capable of withstanding the challenges that mental health issues may bring.

Healthy Habits

Maintaining a balanced lifestyle is crucial for both mental and physical well-being. Developing healthy habits can significantly impact how individuals navigate their personal and professional challenges. In the context of the book 'Her Issues, His Struggles,' understanding the importance of these habits is essential for addressing the unique challenges faced by both genders.

One of the fundamental aspects of cultivating healthy habits is establishing a consistent routine. Routines provide structure, which can help reduce stress and anxiety. By scheduling regular activities such as exercise, meals, and relaxation, individuals can create a sense of control over their lives. This predictability can be particularly beneficial for those dealing with unpredictable challenges, offering a stable foundation to fall back on.

Nutrition plays a pivotal role in maintaining health. A well-balanced diet not only fuels the body but also supports cognitive function and emotional stability. Consuming a variety of nutrients can help in managing mood swings, enhancing concentration, and boosting energy levels. It's important to incorporate a mix of fruits, vegetables, lean proteins, and whole grains into daily meals. For those facing specific gender-related health issues, such as hormonal imbalances, adjusting dietary choices can make a significant difference in overall well-being.

Physical activity is another cornerstone of healthy living. Regular exercise has been shown to alleviate symptoms of depression and anxiety, improve sleep quality, and enhance self-esteem. Whether it's a daily walk, yoga session, or gym workout, incorporating movement into daily routines can provide both immediate and long-term benefits. Physical activity also fosters resilience, helping individuals to cope better with stress and adversity.

Sleep is often overlooked but is essential for maintaining health. Quality sleep allows the body to repair itself and the brain to process information effectively. Lack of sleep can lead to a host of problems including impaired judgment, reduced immune function, and increased susceptibility to stress. Establishing a regular sleep schedule and creating a restful environment can promote better sleep hygiene, contributing to overall health.

Mental health is equally important in the pursuit of healthy habits. Practices such as mindfulness, meditation, and deep-breathing exercises can help manage stress and improve mental clarity. These practices encourage individuals to remain present and focused, reducing the impact of external pressures. By prioritizing mental health, individuals can increase their resilience against the struggles they face.

Social connections also play a vital role in maintaining health. Building and nurturing relationships can provide emotional support, enhance feelings of belonging, and improve self-worth. Engaging in community activities or maintaining regular contact with friends and family can offer a valuable support network.

Incorporating these healthy habits into daily life requires commitment and perseverance. It's about making conscious choices that lead to a healthier, more balanced lifestyle. By understanding and implementing these practices, individuals can better equip themselves to handle the issues and struggles highlighted in 'Her Issues, His

Struggles.' As they integrate these habits, they pave the way for improved health and well-being, ultimately enhancing their ability to face life's challenges.

Seeking Help

In the complex tapestry of relationships, recognizing when to seek help is a crucial step that can lead to meaningful resolutions and stronger bonds. Often, individuals may find themselves entangled in patterns of behavior or communication that hinder their ability to connect effectively with their partners. Understanding the importance of seeking external assistance can be transformative, offering new perspectives and tools for navigating the challenges that arise.

Many people hesitate to seek help due to various reasons, including stigma, fear of judgment, or the belief that they should be able to solve their problems independently. However, acknowledging the need for help is not a sign of weakness but rather a proactive approach to fostering a healthier relationship. Professional guidance can provide a safe space for individuals to express their concerns and emotions without fear of repercussions.

Therapists and counselors are trained to facilitate conversations that might be difficult to initiate on one's own. They can help identify underlying issues that may not be immediately apparent and offer strategies for addressing them. For instance, in a relationship where communication has broken down, a counselor might introduce techniques for active listening and empathetic dialogue, enabling both partners to feel heard and understood.

Moreover, seeking help can uncover personal growth opportunities. Individuals often carry past experiences and unresolved issues into their relationships, which can manifest as conflicts or misunderstandings. Through therapy, one can gain insights into these personal narratives and learn how they influence current behaviors and interactions. This self-awareness is a powerful tool in transforming negative patterns into positive ones.

In addition to individual or couple's therapy, support groups can also be beneficial. These groups provide a platform for sharing experiences and learning from others who are facing similar challenges. The sense of community and mutual support can be incredibly reassuring, reducing feelings of isolation and offering practical advice from those who have navigated similar struggles.

It is essential to approach the process of seeking help with an open mind and a willingness to change. Resistance to change can be a significant barrier to progress, but embracing new ideas and being receptive to feedback can lead to substantial improvements in personal and relational dynamics. Establishing clear goals and maintaining a commitment to the process can also enhance the effectiveness of the help received.

Ultimately, the decision to seek help should be viewed as an investment in the relationship's future. By addressing issues with the guidance of a professional, individuals can develop a deeper understanding of themselves and their partners, paving the way for a more harmonious and fulfilling partnership. In the broader context, normalizing the act of seeking help can contribute to healthier societal attitudes towards mental and emotional well-being, encouraging more people to take proactive steps in their personal lives.

Chapter 8: Educational Disparities

Access to Education

Education serves as a cornerstone for individual empowerment and societal progress, yet access to education remains a significant challenge for many, particularly women and girls. Societal norms, economic barriers, and institutional policies often create obstacles that hinder the educational attainment of females compared to their male counterparts. These disparities in access to education not only impact personal development but also have broader implications for community and national growth.

Historically, cultural expectations and gender roles have dictated the extent to which females can pursue education. In many regions, especially in developing countries, education for girls is not prioritized. Families may allocate limited resources to educate sons rather than daughters, reflecting a belief that males will provide greater economic returns in the future. This mindset is perpetuated by traditional gender roles, where women are expected to focus on domestic responsibilities rather than formal education and professional careers. Such cultural barriers are deeply ingrained, making it difficult to shift perspectives and prioritize education for all children, regardless of gender.

Economic factors also play a crucial role in determining access to education. Families with limited financial resources often face tough decisions about which children to send to school. The costs associated with education, including school fees, uniforms, and supplies, can be prohibitive for low-income families. In areas where public education is not freely accessible, these costs can create insurmountable barriers for families struggling to meet basic needs. Additionally, girls may be required to contribute to household income through labor, further reducing their opportunities to attend school regularly.

Institutional policies and practices can either mitigate or exacerbate educational inequalities. In some cases, schools may lack adequate facilities, such as separate restrooms for girls, which can deter female attendance. Furthermore, the curriculum and teaching methods may not be inclusive or sensitive to the unique challenges faced by girls, leading to disengagement and dropout. Teacher biases and discriminatory practices can also discourage girls from pursuing their education, particularly in subjects traditionally dominated by males, such as science and mathematics.

Despite these challenges, numerous efforts are underway to improve access to education for girls and women. International organizations, governments, and non-governmental organizations are working collaboratively to address these barriers. Initiatives include providing scholarships, building schools in remote areas, and implementing policies that promote gender equality in education. Programs that focus on community awareness and engagement are also crucial, as they help shift cultural perceptions about the value of educating girls.

Moreover, technology is emerging as a powerful tool to bridge educational gaps. Online learning platforms and digital resources can provide access to quality education for those in underserved regions. These technological advancements offer flexible learning opportunities and can be particularly beneficial for girls who may face constraints in attending traditional schools.

Enhancing access to education for girls is not just a matter of social justice but also a strategic investment in the future.

Educated women are more likely to contribute positively to their families, communities, and economies. By dismantling the barriers to education, societies can unlock the potential of millions of girls and women, fostering a more equitable and prosperous world for all.

Educational Attainment

In the complex landscape of gender dynamics, educational attainment plays a pivotal role in shaping the experiences and opportunities available to individuals. It acts as a crucial determinant of socioeconomic status, influencing not only career prospects but also impacting personal and societal levels of empowerment and equality. For women, educational attainment often represents a pathway to independence and self-sufficiency, offering tools and knowledge that can help navigate societal expectations and challenges. Despite significant progress in recent decades, disparities in educational attainment between genders continue to exist, influenced by a myriad of cultural, economic, and policy-related factors.

Globally, girls and women are increasingly gaining access to education, with enrollment rates in primary and secondary education showing remarkable improvements. However, the transition to higher education and the completion rates for women still lag behind in many regions. Factors such as early marriage, cultural norms, and economic constraints often hinder women's educational pursuits. In many societies, traditional gender roles prioritize domestic responsibilities over educational ambitions for women, creating a barrier to their academic advancement. This systemic issue not only limits women's potential but also perpetuates cycles of dependency and inequality.

On the other hand, men's struggles with educational attainment often manifest in different ways. In several developed countries, there is a growing concern about the declining enrollment rates of men in higher education. This trend can be attributed to various factors, including societal perceptions of masculinity, which may devalue academic achievement in favor of immediate financial gain or labor-intensive careers. Additionally, educational systems that fail to engage boys effectively or address their unique learning needs contribute to higher dropout rates and lower academic performance among male students.

The intersection of educational attainment with gender roles also has profound implications for family dynamics and economic stability. Women with higher educational levels tend to have fewer children, marry later, and contribute significantly to household income, thereby altering traditional family structures. This shift can lead to empowerment and increased agency for women within their families and communities. Conversely, men with lower educational attainment may face challenges in securing stable, well-paying jobs, which can affect their ability to fulfill conventional expectations as primary breadwinners.

Policies aimed at addressing these disparities often emphasize the importance of inclusive and equitable education systems. Gender-sensitive educational policies and practices, such as providing scholarships for girls, implementing mentorship programs, and creating supportive learning environments, are crucial in promoting equal opportunities. For men, interventions may focus on redefining masculinity, encouraging academic engagement, and providing career counseling and support to prevent early school leaving.

Ultimately, educational attainment is more than just an individual achievement; it is a societal asset that drives progress and innovation. By addressing the gender-specific challenges and barriers within educational systems, societies can harness the full potential of their populations, fostering environments where both women and men can thrive and contribute meaningfully to their communities. Through collective efforts and a commitment to equity, the transformative power of education can be realized, paving the way for a more just and balanced world.

Learning Styles

Understanding the diverse ways in which individuals learn can significantly impact how they process and retain information. In the context of 'Her Issues, His Struggles,' it is crucial to explore how learning styles can influence the dynamics between individuals, particularly in relationships where personal growth and communication are key components. Learning styles are essentially the preferred approaches individuals use to absorb, process, and comprehend information. Recognizing these styles can aid in fostering better communication, empathy, and understanding between partners.

First, consider the visual learning style, where individuals prefer to use images, diagrams, and spatial understanding to comprehend information. People who are visual learners often benefit from seeing information presented in a way that they can visualize. In relationships, this can translate into using visual aids, such as charts or diagrams, to discuss issues or plan future goals. Visual learners may also appreciate written notes or messages more than verbal communication, as they can process and reflect on these in their own time.

Auditory learners, on the other hand, thrive on listening. They prefer to hear information and often excel in environments where they can engage in discussions and listen to lectures or talks. For auditory learners, communication in relationships may be more effective when issues are discussed openly and verbally. They may find it easier to express emotions and understand their partner when conversations are held face-to-face or over the phone rather than through text.

Kinesthetic learners prefer a hands-on approach. They learn best by doing and often find it challenging to sit still for long periods. In relationships, kinesthetic learners might benefit from activities that involve physical engagement, such as working on a project together or participating in shared hobbies. These activities not only help them process information but also strengthen the bond between partners through shared experiences.

Reading/Writing learners gravitate towards interaction with text. They enjoy reading and writing as their primary method for absorbing information. In relationships, these learners might prefer to communicate through written letters, emails, or even journaling. They often appreciate when their partner takes the time to write down thoughts or plans, as it allows them to process the information at their own pace.

Identifying and understanding these different learning styles can help partners support each other's personal and emotional growth. By tailoring communication and activities to fit each other's learning preferences, couples can enhance their interactions and reduce misunderstandings. It is important to remember that most people do not fit neatly into one category; instead, they may exhibit a combination of learning styles. Therefore, flexibility and openness to trying different approaches are essential in accommodating each other's needs.

Ultimately, awareness of learning styles extends beyond personal growth and can be a valuable tool in any relationship. It encourages empathy and patience, as partners strive to understand not just what is being communicated, but how it is being processed by the other person. This understanding can lead to more effective communication strategies, fostering a deeper connection and mutual respect between partners.

Lifelong Learning

In a rapidly changing world, the concept of lifelong learning has evolved from a luxury to a necessity. This perpetual educational process is crucial for both personal fulfillment and professional advancement. For women, the pursuit of lifelong learning can often be intertwined with societal expectations and personal responsibilities, creating a unique set of challenges and opportunities. Meanwhile, men may face their own hurdles in adapting to new learning paradigms, especially those that deviate from traditional educational pathways. The commitment to lifelong learning requires a continuous effort to acquire new knowledge and skills, which can empower individuals to navigate the complexities of modern life more effectively.

Women, historically, have had to balance multiple roles, often prioritizing family and caregiving over personal development. This balancing act can result in limited opportunities for formal education or professional growth. However, the digital age has opened up new avenues for women to engage in lifelong learning. Online courses, webinars, and digital resources offer flexible learning options that can be tailored to fit into busy schedules. This accessibility allows women to pursue interests and develop skills without sacrificing other responsibilities, fostering a sense of empowerment and independence.

Men, on the other hand, might encounter societal expectations that discourage them from seeking help or admitting gaps in their knowledge. Traditional notions of masculinity often emphasize self-reliance and expertise, which can hinder the willingness to engage in lifelong learning. However, as industries evolve and demand new skills, the pressure to adapt becomes unavoidable. Men may find themselves needing to upskill or reskill to remain competitive in the job market. Embracing lifelong learning can challenge these traditional norms, encouraging a culture of growth and adaptability.

Both genders can benefit from the diverse perspectives and skillsets that lifelong learning fosters. Engaging in a continuous learning process can lead to improved problem-solving abilities, enhanced creativity, and greater resilience. It also equips individuals with the tools needed to navigate the ever-changing landscape of technology, economy, and society. Furthermore, lifelong learning can promote mental well-being by keeping the mind active and engaged, reducing the risk of cognitive decline.

Organizations and educational institutions play a significant role in facilitating lifelong learning. By providing access to resources, training programs, and mentorship opportunities, they can support individuals in their learning journeys. Employers, in particular, can benefit from encouraging a culture of continuous learning, as it leads to a more skilled and adaptable workforce. Policies that support work-life balance and provide educational benefits can make lifelong learning more attainable for everyone.

In essence, lifelong learning is not just about acquiring new skills or knowledge; it is about fostering a mindset that values growth, adaptability, and self-improvement. By embracing this mindset, individuals can transcend traditional roles and expectations, paving the way for personal and professional success. As both men and women navigate the challenges and opportunities of lifelong learning, they contribute to a more dynamic and inclusive society. The journey of lifelong learning is unique for each person, yet it is a shared endeavor that holds the potential to transform lives and communities.

Chapter 9: Relationship Dynamics

Trust and Commitment

In any relationship, the foundations of trust and commitment are essential for ensuring a healthy and enduring partnership. Trust, a fundamental element, acts as the glue that holds two people together, allowing them to rely on each other and feel secure within the relationship. It is the belief that one's partner will act in the best interest of both parties, honoring agreements and maintaining honesty. Trust is not built overnight; it develops over time through consistent actions, open communication, and mutual respect.

Commitment, on the other hand, refers to the dedication and willingness to work through challenges and stay together despite difficulties. It involves a conscious decision to prioritize the relationship and invest time and effort into nurturing it. Commitment is demonstrated through loyalty, perseverance, and the ability to compromise when necessary. Both partners must be willing to make sacrifices and work collaboratively to overcome obstacles that may arise.

The interplay between trust and commitment is crucial, as each reinforces the other. Trust fosters a sense of safety and confidence, which encourages individuals to commit fully to the relationship. When trust is present, partners are more likely to feel secure in their commitment, knowing that their efforts will be reciprocated and valued. Conversely, a strong commitment can enhance trust, as it shows a partner's dedication to maintaining the relationship, even during challenging times.

However, building and maintaining trust and commitment can be challenging, particularly when past experiences or external factors create doubt or insecurity. Previous betrayals or disappointments may lead individuals to be cautious, making it difficult to fully trust or commit. In such cases, open and honest communication becomes vital. Partners should express their feelings and concerns, allowing for a deeper understanding of each other's perspectives and fostering a supportive environment.

Moreover, consistency in actions plays a significant role in reinforcing trust and commitment. Consistently demonstrating reliability, honesty, and integrity helps partners feel confident in their relationship. When actions align with words, it becomes easier to trust and commit, as there are fewer discrepancies or uncertainties. Furthermore, acknowledging and appreciating each other's efforts can strengthen the bond, as it reinforces the value placed on the relationship.

It's important to recognize that trust and commitment are ongoing processes that require attention and effort. They are not static but evolve as the relationship progresses. Regularly assessing the state of trust and commitment can help identify areas that may need improvement or reinforcement. Engaging in activities that build connection, such as spending quality time together or sharing meaningful experiences, can also enhance trust and commitment.

In situations where trust is broken, rebuilding it necessitates patience, understanding, and a willingness to forgive. Both partners must be committed to the process, acknowledging the hurt and working towards healing. Reaffirming commitment through consistent actions and open dialogue can gradually restore trust.

Ultimately, trust and commitment are integral components of a successful relationship. By cultivating these elements, partners can create a strong foundation that supports growth, resilience, and mutual fulfillment. As trust and commitment deepen, they pave the way for a more harmonious and enduring partnership.

Love Languages

Understanding the concept of love languages is crucial for navigating the complexities of relationships. Love languages, a term popularized by Dr. Gary Chapman, refer to the different ways individuals express and receive love. These are Words of Affirmation, Acts of Service, Receiving Gifts, Quality Time, and Physical Touch. Each person has a unique preference, and recognizing this can significantly enhance mutual understanding and communication in relationships.

Words of Affirmation focus on verbal expressions of affection. Compliments, words of appreciation, and verbal encouragement are central to this love language. Individuals who favor this method value hearing "I love you" or receiving positive affirmations. This is not just about flattery but about genuine expressions that reinforce their sense of being loved and valued.

Acts of Service emphasize actions over words. For those who resonate with this language, simple acts like cooking a meal, helping with chores, or running errands demonstrate love more powerfully than words. It is the effort and thoughtfulness behind these actions that convey deep affection and commitment.

Receiving Gifts is not about materialism but about the thoughtfulness and effort behind the gift. For some, tangible symbols of love are important. These gifts serve as a visual representation of love and thought. It's not the monetary value but the symbolic meaning and the intention behind the gift that makes it significant.

Quality Time involves giving undivided attention to one's partner. It's about being present and engaging with each other without distractions. This could be through meaningful conversations, shared activities, or simply enjoying each other's company. For those who favor this language, being together and attentive is the ultimate way of showing love.

Physical Touch encompasses more than just sexual intimacy. It includes holding hands, hugging, kissing, and other forms of physical connection. For individuals who prioritize this love language, physical presence and accessibility are crucial. This form of expression communicates warmth, safety, and love.

Understanding these love languages can help partners express their love in ways that resonate deeply with each other. Misunderstandings often arise when partners have different love language preferences and fail to recognize or appreciate the other's expressions of love. For instance, one partner may express love through Acts of Service, while the other yearns for Words of Affirmation. This mismatch can lead to feelings of neglect or unappreciation if not addressed.

To bridge this gap, it is essential for partners to communicate openly about their love languages and make conscious efforts to express love in ways that are meaningful to each other. This may involve learning and adapting to each other's preferences, which can strengthen the emotional bond and foster a more fulfilling relationship. By acknowledging and respecting each other's love languages, couples can navigate through their issues and struggles with greater empathy and understanding, ultimately enhancing their connection and intimacy. Recognizing and valuing each other's unique love languages is a step toward building a resilient and supportive partnership.

Handling Conflicts

In any relationship, conflicts are inevitable. They arise from differences in personality, perspectives, goals, and even day-to-day habits. Understanding how to handle these conflicts effectively is crucial for maintaining a healthy and harmonious partnership. The first step in handling conflicts is recognizing that they are a normal part of any relationship. This acknowledgment helps in reducing the stigma or fear associated with disagreements. Once both partners accept that conflicts are natural, they can approach these situations with a mindset geared towards resolution rather than confrontation.

Effective communication is the cornerstone of resolving conflicts. It involves not only expressing one's feelings and concerns clearly but also actively listening to the partner's viewpoint. Active listening requires patience and empathy, allowing each person to feel heard and understood. When individuals feel that their perspective is valued, they are more likely to engage in constructive dialogue rather than defensive arguments.

Another vital aspect of handling conflicts is maintaining respect for each other. Even in the heat of an argument, it is essential to avoid insults, sarcasm, or any form of disrespect. These behaviors can escalate the conflict and cause long-term damage to the relationship. Instead, focusing on the issue at hand and addressing it with respect can lead to a more productive outcome. This involves using 'I' statements to express feelings, such as 'I feel hurt when...' instead of blaming the partner with 'You always...'.

Finding common ground is also crucial in resolving conflicts. This means identifying shared goals or values that both partners can agree upon. By focusing on these commonalities, couples can work together to find solutions that satisfy both parties. Compromise often plays a significant role in this process. It requires both individuals to be flexible and open-minded, willing to make concessions for the greater good of the relationship.

Additionally, it is important to choose the right time and place to discuss conflicts. Attempting to resolve issues in the middle of a stressful day or in public can lead to heightened emotions and less effective communication. Setting aside dedicated time to talk in a calm and private environment can facilitate a more rational and thoughtful discussion.

It is also beneficial for couples to develop problem-solving skills together. This can involve brainstorming potential solutions together, evaluating the pros and cons of each option, and collaboratively deciding on the best course of action. By approaching conflicts as a team, partners can strengthen their bond and improve their ability to handle future disagreements.

Finally, it is important to recognize when external help might be necessary. Some conflicts may be too complex or emotionally charged for a couple to handle on their own. In such cases, seeking the guidance of a therapist or counselor can provide valuable insights and strategies for resolution. Professional support can offer a neutral perspective and equip couples with the tools needed to navigate their conflicts more effectively.

Ultimately, the way conflicts are handled can significantly impact the overall health of a relationship. By approaching disagreements with understanding, respect, and a willingness to work together, couples can not only resolve their issues but also grow stronger through the process.

Growth Together

In the complex tapestry of relationships, growth is an essential thread that weaves two individuals together, fostering a deeper understanding and a stronger bond. Growth together is not merely about individual development; it is a dynamic process that involves mutual support, shared experiences, and collective resilience. This subchapter delves into the intricacies of how couples can cultivate growth in their relationship, overcoming personal challenges while nurturing their connection.

The foundation of growing together lies in open communication. For partners to evolve as a unit, they must be able to express their thoughts, fears, and aspirations without fear of judgment. This openness creates a safe space where both individuals can explore their personal issues and struggles, knowing they have a supportive partner by their side. Effective communication helps in identifying areas of growth and establishing common goals that align with the couple's shared vision.

Another critical aspect is the willingness to adapt and change. Relationships require flexibility, as life brings various challenges and opportunities that demand adaptability. When both partners are open to change, they can better support each other's growth journeys. This adaptability also involves recognizing and appreciating each other's differences, which can be a source of strength rather than discord. By valuing diverse perspectives, couples can learn from each other and incorporate new ways of thinking and being into their relationship.

Shared experiences play a significant role in fostering growth. Whether it's traveling to new places, engaging in a new hobby, or facing life's challenges together, shared experiences create memories and deepen the connection between partners. These experiences provide opportunities to learn from each other, discover new facets of their personalities, and build a reservoir of positive moments that can be drawn upon during difficult times.

Support is another cornerstone of growing together. This involves being there for each other during times of need, offering encouragement, and celebrating each other's achievements. Supportive partners help each other overcome personal struggles by providing a listening ear, giving constructive feedback, and sometimes simply being present. This support reinforces the idea that neither partner is alone in their journey, fostering a sense of belonging and security.

Lastly, the concept of shared goals is pivotal. When couples work towards common objectives, they create a sense of unity and purpose. These goals can range from personal aspirations, such as career advancement or personal development, to joint endeavors like building a family or achieving financial stability. By aligning their efforts towards these goals, couples can motivate each other and hold each other accountable, ensuring that both partners are committed to their shared vision.

Growing together as a couple is a continuous process that requires effort, patience, and understanding. It involves navigating personal and relational challenges while maintaining a focus on mutual development. By prioritizing communication, adaptability, shared experiences, support, and common goals, couples can create a solid foundation for their relationship, allowing them to face life's challenges as a united front and emerge stronger than before.

Chapter 10: Parenting Pressures

Raising Children

Raising children presents a unique set of challenges and joys that require both parents to navigate a complex landscape of responsibilities and expectations. This intricate task demands a blend of patience, understanding, and collaboration between partners, as they strive to create a nurturing environment that fosters the growth and development of their children. The dynamics of parenting have evolved significantly over the years, influenced by cultural shifts and changing societal norms, yet the core principles of love, support, and guidance remain steadfast.

Central to effective parenting is the ability to communicate openly and constructively. Parents must engage in ongoing dialogue to align their values and strategies, ensuring a unified approach to discipline, education, and emotional support. This collaboration not only strengthens the parental bond but also provides children with a stable and consistent framework within which they can thrive. Effective communication also involves listening to the children's perspectives, understanding their needs, and adapting parenting styles to accommodate individual differences.

Balancing work and family life is another critical aspect of raising children that often requires careful negotiation between partners. As more families have dual-income parents, the challenge of allocating time and energy to both professional and domestic responsibilities becomes more pronounced. Parents must work together to establish routines that allow for quality family time while also meeting their professional obligations. This balance is essential for modeling a healthy work-life integration for children, teaching them the importance of time management and prioritization.

The role of technology in modern parenting is a double-edged sword that offers both opportunities and challenges. On one hand, technology can be a valuable tool for education and entertainment, providing children with access to a wealth of information and learning resources. On the other hand, it presents risks related to screen time, online safety, and the potential for digital addiction. Parents must navigate these challenges by setting appropriate boundaries and ensuring that technology use is balanced with other aspects of life, such as physical activity and face-to-face interactions.

Moreover, the mental and emotional well-being of children is a critical component of effective parenting. Parents must be attuned to their children's emotional needs, providing support and guidance as they navigate the complexities of growing up. This involves fostering an environment where children feel safe to express their feelings and concerns, and where they can develop resilience and coping skills to handle life's challenges.

In raising children, the importance of leading by example cannot be overstated. Children learn a great deal by observing their parents' behavior, attitudes, and interactions with others. Demonstrating empathy, responsibility, and integrity in everyday actions instills these values in children, helping them to develop into compassionate and conscientious individuals. Ultimately, the collaborative effort of parenting not only shapes the next generation but also strengthens the bond between partners, creating a supportive and loving family unit.

Balancing Roles

In modern relationships, the division of roles and responsibilities often becomes a focal point of discussion. The dynamics of balancing roles in a partnership can be complex, as they are influenced by cultural, societal, and personal factors. Historically, there were clear delineations between the roles of men and women, with each gender having specific expectations and duties. However, as society evolves, these traditional roles are being redefined, creating both opportunities and challenges for couples striving to find equilibrium in their relationships.

One significant factor influencing the balancing of roles is the shift in gender norms. As women increasingly participate in the workforce and men take on more active roles in domestic life, couples are tasked with negotiating new boundaries and responsibilities. This shift necessitates open communication and a willingness to adapt. Partners must engage in honest conversations about expectations and workloads, ensuring that neither feels overburdened or undervalued.

Another aspect to consider is the individual strengths and interests of each partner. Balancing roles does not mean an equal division of tasks but rather an equitable one. Couples should assess their unique skills and preferences when determining who takes on specific duties. For instance, one partner may excel in financial management, while the other may have a knack for organizing and planning. By leveraging these strengths, couples can create a dynamic that benefits both parties and enhances the relationship.

The importance of flexibility cannot be overstated in the context of role balancing. Life is unpredictable, and circumstances can change rapidly. Whether due to career shifts, health issues, or family needs, partners must be prepared to reassess and redistribute roles as necessary. Flexibility allows couples to respond to these changes without resentment or conflict, fostering a supportive and resilient partnership.

Additionally, societal pressures and stereotypes can impact the way roles are balanced within a relationship. External expectations can create stress and tension, particularly when they conflict with the couple's personal values or desires. It is crucial for partners to actively challenge these stereotypes and prioritize their own understanding of what works best for them. By focusing on their unique dynamic rather than conforming to societal norms, couples can create a more authentic and fulfilling partnership.

Effective communication is the cornerstone of successfully balancing roles. Regular check-ins and discussions about responsibilities, feelings, and expectations can prevent misunderstandings and ensure that both partners feel heard and appreciated. This ongoing dialogue helps to maintain a balance that evolves with the relationship, accommodating changes and growth over time.

Ultimately, balancing roles in a relationship is an ongoing process that requires effort, understanding, and compromise. It involves a continuous evaluation of each partner's contributions and needs, as well as a commitment to supporting one another. By embracing these principles, couples can navigate the complexities of modern relationships, creating a partnership that is both equitable and satisfying.

Educational Choices

In the complex landscape of modern education, individuals face a myriad of choices that significantly impact their personal and professional trajectories. Educational choices are pivotal, as they shape not only career paths but also influence personal development and societal contribution. This subchapter delves into the multifaceted nature of these decisions, exploring the various factors that influence them and the potential outcomes they yield.

The first consideration in educational choices often revolves around the selection of a field of study. This decision is typically influenced by personal interests, perceived strengths, and career aspirations. Students frequently grapple with the dilemma of pursuing a passion versus opting for a field with robust job prospects. While some are driven by intrinsic motivations and the desire for personal fulfillment, others prioritize financial stability and job security. This dichotomy highlights the tension between following one's interests and making practical choices that align with economic realities.

Another critical factor in educational choices is the type of institution. Prospective students weigh the benefits of attending prestigious universities against the potential advantages of smaller, specialized colleges or vocational schools. The decision is often informed by considerations such as the quality of education, networking opportunities, and the institution's perceived prestige in the job market. Additionally, financial constraints and the availability of scholarships or financial aid play a significant role in determining the feasibility of attending certain institutions.

Geographical location also plays a crucial role in educational decisions. Students may choose to study in urban centers that offer diverse opportunities and cultural experiences, or they may opt for institutions in rural areas that provide a quieter, more focused learning environment. The location can influence not only the educational experience but also post-graduation employment opportunities, as some regions have a higher demand for certain skill sets.

Moreover, the mode of education—traditional in-person classes versus online learning—has become an increasingly relevant consideration. The rise of digital technology and the global shift towards virtual learning environments offer flexibility and accessibility, allowing individuals to balance education with other commitments. However, this mode of learning may lack the interpersonal interactions and campus experiences that traditional settings provide, which are crucial for developing soft skills and building professional networks.

The decision-making process is further complicated by the rapidly changing job market, influenced by technological advancements and economic shifts. Fields that are in high demand today may not hold the same significance in the future, making it imperative for individuals to remain adaptable and open to lifelong learning. This uncertainty necessitates a strategic approach to education, where individuals not only focus on acquiring specific knowledge but also develop critical thinking, problem-solving, and adaptability skills that are transferable across various fields.

Ultimately, educational choices are deeply personal and influenced by a combination of individual aspirations, external pressures, and societal trends. They require careful consideration of both immediate and long-term implications, balancing personal fulfillment with practical realities. As individuals navigate these decisions, they contribute to shaping their identities and the roles they will play in the broader societal context.

Future Planning

In the intricate dance of life, planning for the future can often feel like an overwhelming task, fraught with uncertainties and potential pitfalls. Yet, it remains an essential component of navigating the complexities of personal and professional relationships. For individuals who find themselves grappling with unique challenges, whether they stem from personal issues or shared struggles, future planning becomes even more critical. Understanding how to effectively plan for the future requires a comprehensive approach that considers both individual aspirations and mutual goals.

The first step in effective future planning is self-assessment. This involves a deep introspection into one's personal values, desires, and long-term goals. It is important for individuals to identify what truly matters to them, both personally and professionally. This self-awareness forms the foundation upon which future plans are built. By understanding what drives them, individuals can make more informed decisions that align with their core values.

Equally important is the need for open and honest communication with partners or collaborators. Whether in a personal relationship or a professional setting, clear communication about expectations, ambitions, and concerns is vital. This dialogue should be ongoing, allowing both parties to express their thoughts and feelings without fear of judgment. This not only helps in aligning goals but also fosters a sense of mutual understanding and support.

Once there is clarity on individual and shared goals, the next step is to set realistic and achievable objectives. This involves breaking down larger goals into smaller, manageable tasks that can be accomplished progressively over time. Setting specific, measurable, achievable, relevant, and time-bound (SMART) goals can be particularly helpful. This approach ensures that progress can be tracked and adjustments made as needed, keeping the plan flexible and adaptable to changing circumstances.

Financial planning is another critical component of future planning. Whether it involves budgeting for personal expenses, saving for future investments, or planning for unforeseen contingencies, having a solid financial plan can provide a sense of security and stability. It's important to regularly review and adjust financial plans to reflect any changes in income, expenses, or life circumstances.

Moreover, future planning should also consider potential challenges and obstacles. By anticipating possible hurdles, individuals can develop contingency plans that allow them to respond effectively when faced with unexpected situations. This proactive approach reduces the likelihood of being caught off guard and helps maintain momentum towards achieving long-term goals.

Finally, it is essential to periodically review and reflect on the progress of the future plan. This allows individuals to celebrate successes, learn from setbacks, and make necessary adjustments. Regular reflection ensures that the plan remains aligned with evolving goals and circumstances, keeping it relevant and effective.

In essence, future planning is not a one-time event but a continuous process of evaluation, adjustment, and growth. By approaching it with a clear understanding of personal values, open communication, realistic goal-setting, financial foresight, and adaptability, individuals can navigate their unique challenges more effectively. This not only enhances personal fulfillment but also strengthens the bonds in shared endeavors, paving the way for a more harmonious and prosperous future.

Chapter 11: Technology and Relationships

Digital Communication

In the ever-evolving landscape of relationships, digital communication has emerged as a pivotal factor influencing the dynamics between individuals. As technology advances, it offers new avenues for connection, yet simultaneously introduces challenges that can complicate interpersonal interactions. Couples today find themselves navigating a web of texts, emails, and social media interactions, each playing a crucial role in shaping modern relationships.

The convenience and immediacy of digital communication have transformed how partners communicate. Instant messaging and video calls have bridged geographical distances, allowing couples to maintain a sense of closeness even when physically apart. This constant connectivity can enhance the emotional bond, fostering a sense of support and understanding. Partners can share their experiences in real-time, providing an immediacy that was not possible in previous generations.

However, the digital realm also presents challenges. The absence of non-verbal cues, such as tone of voice and body language, can lead to misunderstandings. A message intended to be humorous may be perceived as sarcastic or dismissive, leading to unnecessary conflict. The brevity often required by digital platforms can also result in oversimplification, where complex emotions are reduced to emojis or brief phrases, risking misinterpretation.

Moreover, the allure of social media can introduce issues of privacy and trust. The public nature of platforms like Instagram or Facebook means that aspects of a relationship may be exposed to a wider audience than intended. This exposure can lead to pressure to present an idealized version of the relationship, which might not reflect reality. Additionally, the temptation to compare one's relationship to others, based on curated social media posts, can foster feelings of inadequacy or dissatisfaction.

Digital communication also affects how conflicts are managed within relationships. While technology allows for immediate response and resolution, it can also facilitate avoidance. The ease of ignoring a message or delaying a response can lead to unresolved issues festering beneath the surface. On the other hand, the digital record of conversations can be both a blessing and a curse. While it provides a reference for past discussions, it can also lead to rehashing old arguments, hindering the ability to move forward.

Furthermore, the boundary between personal and digital life is increasingly blurred. Notifications and alerts demand constant attention, often intruding on personal time and space. This intrusion can lead to feelings of being undervalued or neglected when a partner appears more engaged with their device than with their significant other. Establishing boundaries and setting aside technology-free time becomes crucial in maintaining a healthy balance.

Despite these challenges, digital communication offers opportunities for growth and understanding. It requires couples to develop new skills in communication and empathy, fostering resilience and adaptability. By being mindful of the potential pitfalls and actively working to mitigate them, couples can harness the benefits of digital communication to strengthen their relationships. As technology continues to evolve, so too must the strategies employed to navigate its impact on personal connections, ensuring that these tools serve to enhance rather than hinder the bonds between partners.

Social Media Impact

Social media has become an integral part of modern life, influencing the way individuals interact, communicate, and perceive the world around them. Its impact on personal relationships and individual well-being is profound, creating both opportunities and challenges for people navigating their daily lives. This digital landscape offers a platform for self-expression and connection, but it also presents a unique set of pressures and expectations.

One of the most significant effects of social media is its ability to connect people across distances, allowing individuals to maintain relationships regardless of geographical boundaries. It provides a space where people can share experiences, celebrate milestones, and offer support during difficult times. The immediacy of communication fosters a sense of closeness and community, bridging gaps that might otherwise hinder relationships.

However, the constant connectivity facilitated by social media can also lead to feelings of isolation and inadequacy. The curated nature of online profiles often presents an idealized version of reality, leading individuals to compare themselves to others. This comparison can result in decreased self-esteem and increased anxiety, as users may feel pressured to meet unrealistic standards of success, beauty, or happiness. The fear of missing out, commonly referred to as FOMO, can exacerbate these feelings, as individuals may perceive others as living more fulfilling or exciting lives.

Moreover, social media can impact mental health by contributing to a cycle of validation-seeking behavior. The pursuit of likes, comments, and shares can become addictive, with individuals measuring their self-worth by the attention they receive online. This need for external validation can detract from genuine self-acceptance and self-compassion, leading to a reliance on external affirmation for self-esteem.

The impact of social media extends to romantic relationships as well. The ease of communication can enhance intimacy and understanding between partners, providing a platform for sharing thoughts and emotions. However, it can also introduce challenges such as jealousy, miscommunication, and a lack of privacy. The visibility of interactions with others can lead to misunderstandings and conflicts, as partners may misconstrue the intentions behind likes or comments on posts.

Additionally, social media can influence societal norms and expectations, shaping perceptions of gender roles and relationships. The portrayal of idealized relationships can create unrealistic expectations, leading individuals to question the validity and quality of their own partnerships. These depictions can reinforce stereotypes and perpetuate traditional gender roles, impacting how individuals navigate their roles within a relationship.

Despite these challenges, social media also offers opportunities for empowerment and advocacy. It provides a platform for marginalized voices to be heard, fostering awareness and dialogue around critical social issues. Individuals can find communities and support networks that validate their experiences and identities, promoting inclusivity and understanding.

In navigating the complex landscape of social media, individuals must cultivate a balanced approach, recognizing both its potential benefits and pitfalls. By fostering self-awareness and setting boundaries, people can harness the positive aspects of social media while mitigating its negative effects. Ultimately, understanding the impact of social media is essential for maintaining healthy relationships and individual well-being in an increasingly digital world.

Privacy Concerns

In the rapidly evolving digital age, privacy concerns have surged to the forefront of societal discourse, shaping the dynamics of personal relationships. As technology becomes more intertwined with daily life, the lines between public and private spheres blur, introducing new challenges for individuals seeking to maintain their personal boundaries. In the context of relationships, these privacy issues can manifest in various forms, often leading to misunderstandings and conflicts between partners.

One of the primary factors contributing to privacy concerns is the pervasive use of social media platforms. These platforms encourage users to share personal information, often without fully understanding the implications. This sharing culture can lead to an expectation of transparency between partners, which may not always be comfortable or appropriate for both parties. For instance, one partner might feel obliged to share their online interactions or whereabouts, leading to a perceived invasion of privacy and potential friction.

Moreover, the advent of smartphones and other digital devices means that individuals are constantly connected, leaving a digital footprint that is difficult to erase. This connectivity can lead to issues such as digital surveillance, where one partner might feel compelled to monitor the other's activities. This behavior, often rooted in insecurity or mistrust, can erode the foundation of a healthy relationship, as it undermines the essential elements of trust and respect.

Privacy concerns are further exacerbated by the increasing use of smart devices and applications that collect vast amounts of personal data. These technologies, while offering convenience and efficiency, often operate with minimal transparency regarding data collection and usage. Partners may find themselves in conflict over the use of such technologies, particularly if one individual is more concerned about data privacy than the other. This discrepancy can lead to disagreements about what information is shared and with whom, both within the relationship and with external entities.

Additionally, the concept of privacy is subjective and can vary significantly between individuals. Cultural, generational, and personal values all play a role in shaping one's perception of privacy. For example, what one person considers a harmless sharing of information might be seen by another as a breach of personal space. This divergence in privacy expectations can lead to tension and conflict, as partners struggle to navigate the delicate balance between openness and privacy.

To address these privacy concerns, it is crucial for individuals in relationships to engage in open and honest communication. Discussing personal boundaries and privacy expectations can help partners understand each other's comfort levels and establish mutual respect. It is also important for individuals to educate themselves about the technologies they use and the potential privacy implications involved. By doing so, they can make informed decisions about their digital interactions and set appropriate boundaries that align with their values.

As privacy issues continue to evolve alongside technological advancements, couples must remain vigilant and proactive in addressing these challenges. By fostering a culture of trust and open communication, partners can navigate the complexities of privacy concerns and strengthen their relationships in the face of an ever-changing digital landscape.

Technology as a Tool

In the modern age, technology permeates every aspect of our lives, influencing how we communicate, work, and even think. Its role as a tool is multifaceted, offering both opportunities and challenges in navigating personal and professional realms. As we delve into the dynamics of relationships and personal growth, technology emerges as a pivotal element that can either bridge gaps or widen them, depending on its application.

Understanding technology as a tool involves recognizing its dual nature. On one hand, it provides platforms for connection, enabling individuals to maintain relationships across distances and time zones. Social media, video conferencing, and instant messaging have redefined the way we interact, offering immediacy and intimacy that were previously unattainable. These tools can foster deeper connections when used mindfully, allowing for continuous communication that can strengthen bonds.

Conversely, the same tools can create barriers. The illusion of connection through screens can sometimes lead to superficial interactions, depriving relationships of depth and authenticity. Misunderstandings may arise from the absence of non-verbal cues, and the constant availability can lead to burnout or a sense of being overwhelmed. Thus, the challenge lies in leveraging technology to enhance, rather than hinder, genuine connection.

In the professional sphere, technology serves as a catalyst for efficiency and innovation. It streamlines processes, facilitates remote work, and democratizes access to information and resources. For individuals facing struggles in their careers, technology can be an ally, offering tools for skill development and career advancement. Online courses, webinars, and virtual networking events provide avenues for continuous learning and professional growth, allowing individuals to adapt to changing job markets and demands.

However, the rapid pace of technological advancement also necessitates adaptability and resilience. The pressure to keep up with new tools and platforms can be daunting, particularly for those who may not have had early exposure to digital environments. This technological divide can exacerbate existing inequalities, creating additional hurdles for those already facing personal or professional challenges.

The key to harnessing technology effectively lies in intentionality and balance. By setting boundaries and establishing mindful usage practices, individuals can mitigate the negative impacts of technology while reaping its benefits. This might involve setting specific times for digital detox, prioritizing face-to-face interactions when possible, and using technology to complement rather than replace traditional forms of communication.

Moreover, technology can be a powerful tool for self-reflection and personal development. Apps for mindfulness, journaling, and habit tracking offer new ways to explore and understand personal issues and struggles. These tools can provide insights and foster self-awareness, empowering individuals to take proactive steps towards personal growth and fulfillment.

Ultimately, technology, when used wisely, can be a transformative tool in addressing and overcoming the issues and struggles that individuals face. By approaching it with a critical and informed perspective, individuals can navigate its complexities and harness its potential to improve their lives and relationships.

Chapter 12: Personal Growth and Development

Self-Discovery

In the realm of personal development, understanding oneself is often considered the cornerstone of growth. It involves a deep and honest examination of one's thoughts, emotions, and behaviors. This process of introspection is not merely about recognizing one's strengths and weaknesses but also about understanding the underlying motivations and desires that drive actions. Self-discovery is a critical element in navigating the complexities of relationships, particularly in the context of 'Her Issues, His Struggles.' This book delves into the nuances of interpersonal dynamics, highlighting how personal growth is intricately tied to relational harmony.\n\nSelf-discovery requires a willingness to confront uncomfortable truths about oneself. It is a transformative process that encourages individuals to look beyond surface-level perceptions and delve deeper into the core of their identity. This exploration often reveals hidden fears, unresolved conflicts, and unmet needs. By acknowledging these aspects, individuals can begin to address the root causes of their struggles and work towards self-improvement.\n\nIn many cases, the challenges faced in relationships are a reflection of internal conflicts. For instance, issues such as insecurity, jealousy, or communication barriers often stem from a lack of self-awareness. When individuals are unaware of their own emotional triggers or behavioral patterns, they may inadvertently project these onto their partners, leading to misunderstandings and conflict. Therefore, self-discovery serves as a vital tool for fostering healthier relationships by promoting empathy and understanding.\n\nThe process of self-discovery is not a solitary journey. It can be facilitated by various means such as therapy, meditation, or engaging in open dialogues with trusted friends and family. These methods provide individuals with the opportunity to gain new perspectives and insights into their behaviors and thought processes. Moreover, they offer a safe space for individuals to express their vulnerabilities and seek guidance in overcoming personal challenges.\n\nMoreover, self-discovery is an ongoing process that evolves over time. As individuals encounter new experiences and challenges, they may uncover different facets of their personality that were previously unknown. This continuous evolution underscores the importance of maintaining an open and curious mindset. By remaining receptive to change and new information, individuals can adapt and grow in ways that enhance their personal and relational well-being.\n\nIn the context of 'Her Issues, His Struggles,' self-discovery is portrayed as a pivotal step towards resolving interpersonal conflicts. The book emphasizes that understanding oneself is not only beneficial for personal growth but also essential for creating meaningful and lasting connections with others. By fostering a deeper awareness of their own needs and desires, individuals can communicate more effectively and cultivate relationships that are based on mutual respect and understanding.\n\nUltimately, self-discovery empowers individuals to take control of their lives and relationships. It encourages them to take responsibility for their actions and make conscious choices that align with their values and aspirations. Through this process, individuals can transform their struggles into opportunities for growth and create a more fulfilling and harmonious life.

Skill Building

In the dynamic interplay between personal challenges and interpersonal dynamics, skill building emerges as a pivotal element for fostering resilience and understanding. The development of skills serves not only as a mechanism for personal growth but also as a bridge to connect with others more effectively. In the context of addressing the issues faced by women and the struggles encountered by men, cultivating specific skills can lead to improved communication, empathy, and problem-solving capabilities.

The first step in skill building involves identifying the areas that require enhancement. For women, this may include skills related to assertiveness, boundary-setting, and self-confidence. These skills are essential for navigating environments where their voices might be marginalized or undervalued. By building assertiveness, women can articulate their needs and desires more clearly, fostering an environment where their contributions are recognized and respected.

Conversely, men may benefit from developing skills that enhance emotional intelligence and vulnerability. Traditionally, societal norms have discouraged men from expressing emotions openly, leading to internalized struggles and strained relationships. By learning to articulate emotions and engage in open dialogue, men can break free from these constraints, leading to healthier interpersonal relationships and a more profound understanding of their own emotional landscapes.

Effective communication is a universal skill that benefits both genders. It involves not just the ability to express oneself clearly but also the capacity to listen actively and empathetically. Active listening requires individuals to fully engage with the speaker, offering feedback that demonstrates understanding and validation of their perspective. This skill is crucial in resolving conflicts and building trust within relationships.

Problem-solving is another critical skill that can alleviate personal and shared challenges. By approaching problems with a solution-oriented mindset, individuals can collaboratively navigate obstacles, fostering a sense of teamwork and shared purpose. This skill is particularly relevant in partnerships where both parties face distinct yet interconnected challenges. By working together to address these issues, couples can strengthen their bond and create a supportive environment that nurtures growth and resilience.

Furthermore, adaptability is a skill that enables individuals to navigate the ever-changing landscape of personal and relational dynamics. Life is inherently unpredictable, and the ability to adjust to new circumstances with flexibility and grace is invaluable. Whether it involves adapting to new roles within a relationship or responding to external pressures, adaptability allows individuals to maintain equilibrium and continue progressing towards their personal and shared goals.

Skill building is not a solitary endeavor; it often involves seeking resources and support from external sources. This could include engaging with mentors, participating in workshops, or utilizing educational materials designed to enhance specific skills. By taking proactive steps to develop their capabilities, individuals can empower themselves and their partners, creating a ripple effect that extends beyond their personal lives into their communities.

Ultimately, skill building is a continuous process that requires commitment and practice. As individuals hone their skills, they not only address their immediate challenges but also lay the foundation for a more harmonious and fulfilling life. Whether through improved communication, emotional intelligence, or adaptability, the skills developed in this journey are integral to overcoming the issues and struggles that define the human experience.

Setting Goals

Understanding the nuances of setting goals is essential as it forms the foundation for addressing the complexities inherent in relationships. Goals provide a roadmap for individuals and couples alike, helping them navigate through the myriad of challenges they encounter. Whether these challenges stem from personal issues or shared struggles, having clear objectives can significantly enhance the likelihood of overcoming them.

Setting goals begins with introspection. Individuals must first identify what they truly desire from their relationships, both emotionally and practically. This requires a deep dive into personal values, needs, and long-term aspirations. By understanding these elements, individuals can articulate what they want to achieve, thereby creating a vision for their relationship.

Next, it is crucial to differentiate between short-term and long-term goals. Short-term goals focus on immediate improvements or changes that can be implemented quickly. These might include enhancing communication skills, scheduling regular date nights, or addressing specific conflicts that have arisen. On the other hand, long-term goals involve broader aspirations such as building a family, achieving financial stability, or fostering a deeper emotional connection. Both types of goals are vital, as they provide a balanced approach to relationship growth.

Once goals are established, it is important to ensure they are realistic and attainable. Setting goals that are too ambitious can lead to frustration and disappointment, which may exacerbate existing issues. Utilizing the SMART criteria—Specific, Measurable, Achievable, Relevant, and Time-bound—can help in crafting goals that are both practical and motivating. For example, instead of setting a vague goal like "improve communication," a more specific goal would be "have a weekly discussion about our feelings and concerns every Sunday evening."

Communication plays a pivotal role in the goal-setting process. Both partners need to be involved in discussions about their individual and shared goals. This collaborative approach ensures that both parties feel heard and valued, fostering a sense of partnership. Open dialogue about goals can also prevent misunderstandings and align expectations, which is crucial for maintaining harmony and mutual support.

Monitoring progress is another key aspect of effective goal setting. Regularly reviewing and reflecting on the progress made towards achieving goals helps maintain momentum and provides opportunities for adjustments if necessary. It is important to celebrate successes, no matter how small, as this reinforces positive behavior and commitment.

Challenges are inevitable, and setbacks may occur. When they do, it is important to remain flexible and resilient. Re-evaluating goals in light of new circumstances or insights can be beneficial. This adaptability ensures that goals remain relevant and achievable, even as life circumstances change.

Ultimately, setting goals within a relationship requires a delicate balance of individual desires and shared objectives. It involves a continuous process of reflection, communication, and adjustment. By setting clear, realistic goals, individuals and couples can better navigate the complexities of their relationships, leading to greater satisfaction and fulfillment.

Overcoming Barriers

Navigating the complex landscape of relationships often involves facing and overcoming a myriad of barriers. These obstacles can stem from personal insecurities, societal expectations, or even past experiences that cast long shadows over present interactions. Understanding these barriers is the first step in addressing them, and this requires both partners to engage in honest and open communication.

One common barrier is the presence of unrealistic expectations. Often, individuals enter relationships with preconceived notions about what their partner should be like or how the relationship should progress. These expectations can be shaped by cultural narratives, media portrayals, or familial influences, and they can place undue pressure on both individuals. When expectations are not met, disappointment can lead to resentment and conflict. To overcome this, it is crucial for partners to set realistic goals and communicate openly about their desires and needs.

Another significant barrier is the fear of vulnerability. Many people struggle with opening up to others due to past traumas or the fear of being judged. This fear can manifest as emotional distancing or a reluctance to share personal thoughts and feelings. Overcoming this barrier involves creating a safe and supportive environment where both partners feel comfortable expressing themselves without fear of ridicule or rejection. Building trust and understanding takes time and patience, but it is essential for the health of the relationship.

Cultural and societal pressures also play a role in shaping relationship dynamics. Gender roles, for instance, can dictate certain behaviors and expectations that may not align with an individual's true self. These pressures can lead to misunderstandings and conflicts as partners struggle to conform to societal norms while trying to remain authentic. Recognizing these external influences and discussing them openly can help couples navigate them more effectively.

Communication barriers are perhaps the most common yet most overlooked obstacles in relationships. Miscommunication can occur due to differences in communication styles, language barriers, or simply a lack of understanding. It is important for partners to actively listen to one another and to seek clarification when needed. Developing effective communication skills can significantly enhance relationship quality and reduce the likelihood of misunderstandings.

Lastly, past experiences can heavily impact present relationships. Individuals may carry emotional baggage from previous relationships that affect their ability to trust or fully engage with a new partner. It is important for individuals to acknowledge these past experiences and work through them, whether through self-reflection, therapy, or open discussions with their partner. By addressing these issues, individuals can prevent them from hindering their current relationship.

In overcoming these barriers, it is essential for both partners to remain committed to growth and understanding. This involves not only recognizing and addressing individual barriers but also supporting one another in the process. By fostering an environment of mutual respect and empathy, couples can navigate the complexities of their relationships more effectively, ultimately leading to a more fulfilling partnership.

Chapter 13: Finding Common Ground

Shared Values

In any relationship, the foundation upon which it is built significantly influences its longevity and harmony. One of the most crucial elements that contribute to this foundation is the presence of shared values. These are the core principles and beliefs that both partners hold dear, which shape their attitudes and behaviors. Shared values serve as a guiding compass, steering couples through the complexities of life and ensuring that their relationship remains anchored amidst challenges.

Shared values encompass a broad spectrum of beliefs, including cultural, moral, ethical, and even spiritual dimensions. They manifest in various aspects of life, such as financial decisions, parenting styles, and lifestyle choices. When partners share similar values, they are more likely to experience a sense of unity and mutual understanding. This alignment reduces the likelihood of conflicts arising from fundamental differences and promotes a cohesive partnership.

One of the primary benefits of shared values is the enhancement of communication within a relationship. When partners operate from a common set of beliefs, they are better equipped to understand each other's perspectives and motivations. This understanding fosters open dialogue, allowing couples to address issues constructively and collaboratively. Communication becomes more than just an exchange of words; it becomes a meaningful interaction that strengthens the bond between partners.

Moreover, shared values contribute to the development of trust and respect in a relationship. When partners recognize that they are aligned in their core beliefs, they are more likely to trust each other's decisions and actions. This trust is built on the assurance that each partner will act in ways that reflect their shared values, even in the absence of the other. Respect naturally follows, as partners appreciate and honor each other's commitment to their shared principles.

The significance of shared values is also evident in the way couples navigate life's challenges. When faced with difficulties, couples with shared values are more likely to approach problems with a united front. They draw strength from their common beliefs, which serve as a source of resilience and determination. This shared approach not only helps in overcoming obstacles but also reinforces the partnership, as both individuals feel supported and understood.

However, it is important to acknowledge that shared values do not imply identical beliefs or perspectives. Each individual brings their unique experiences and viewpoints to a relationship. The key is finding a balance where both partners' values intersect, allowing for individual expression while maintaining a shared vision. This balance requires ongoing communication and compromise, as couples navigate the evolving landscape of their relationship.

In essence, shared values act as the glue that holds a relationship together. They provide a sense of purpose and direction, enabling couples to build a life that reflects their collective aspirations. By fostering a deep sense of connection and understanding, shared values lay the groundwork for a fulfilling and enduring partnership. As relationships grow and evolve, these shared principles remain a constant, guiding partners through the myriad of experiences that life has to offer.

Building Empathy

Empathy serves as a cornerstone for understanding and resolving the complex dynamics between individuals, especially in the context of relationships where 'Her Issues' and 'His Struggles' often intersect. This emotional capability allows one to step into another's shoes, fostering a deeper understanding of their feelings and perspectives. For many, developing empathy requires conscious effort and practice, as it involves setting aside one's own emotions and biases to genuinely comprehend another's experience.

The process of building empathy begins with active listening. This involves more than just hearing words; it requires paying attention to the speaker's tone, body language, and emotional cues. Active listening demands patience and the willingness to withhold judgment, creating a safe space for the speaker to express themselves openly. By doing so, individuals can uncover underlying issues that may not be immediately apparent, thus facilitating a more profound understanding.

Another critical aspect of building empathy is cultivating emotional awareness, both of oneself and others. Recognizing one's own emotional responses can prevent them from clouding judgment or interfering with the ability to empathize. Similarly, being attuned to the emotions of others can provide insights into their behavior and motivations. Emotional awareness is closely linked to emotional regulation, which involves managing one's emotional reactions to maintain a balanced and empathetic approach in interactions.

Practicing perspective-taking is also essential in building empathy. This involves consciously trying to see a situation from another person's viewpoint. It requires imagination and an open mind, as it involves temporarily setting aside one's own perspective to understand another's. Perspective-taking can reveal the nuances of 'Her Issues' and 'His Struggles,' highlighting the unique challenges each faces and the potential for mutual understanding and support.

Empathy is further strengthened by developing a sense of curiosity about others. This involves asking questions and showing genuine interest in another person's experiences and feelings. Curiosity can bridge gaps in understanding and build connections, as it encourages individuals to learn more about each other beyond surface-level interactions. It is important, however, to ensure that this curiosity is respectful and considerate, avoiding intrusive or insensitive questioning.

Moreover, empathy is not a static trait but a skill that can be developed and refined over time. Engaging in activities that promote empathetic understanding, such as reading literature, participating in role-playing exercises, or volunteering, can enhance one's capacity for empathy. These activities expose individuals to diverse perspectives and experiences, broadening their understanding and empathy for others.

In relationships, empathy can transform conflicts into opportunities for growth and connection. By understanding and validating each other's feelings and experiences, partners can address 'Her Issues' and 'His Struggles' collaboratively, fostering a sense of partnership and mutual support. Empathy lays the foundation for effective communication, trust, and emotional intimacy, essential components of any healthy relationship. Ultimately, empathy is a powerful tool that can bridge divides, heal wounds, and strengthen bonds, making it an invaluable asset in navigating the complexities of human relationships.

Collaborative Efforts

In the realm of human relationships, the interplay between individual challenges and collective growth often defines the journey shared by partners. The dynamics between personal issues and mutual struggles can become a tapestry that weaves stronger connections when approached with a collaborative mindset. This subchapter explores how individuals can navigate their unique challenges while fostering a spirit of cooperation and unity within their relationships.\n\nUnderstanding the significance of collaboration requires acknowledging that every individual brings a distinct set of experiences, perspectives, and issues into a relationship. These can range from deeply rooted personal insecurities to external pressures such as career demands or familial expectations. Recognizing these elements as part of a broader narrative allows partners to develop empathy and understanding, forming the foundation for collaborative efforts.\n\nEffective communication stands as a cornerstone of collaborative relationships. It involves more than just exchanging words; it is about actively listening, validating each other's feelings, and engaging in open dialogues. When partners communicate openly, they create an environment where both parties feel heard and valued. This not only helps in addressing immediate issues but also strengthens the relational bond over time.\n\nBeyond communication, setting shared goals can significantly enhance the collaborative efforts within a relationship. Whether these goals are related to personal growth, financial stability, or achieving work-life balance, having a common objective helps partners align their actions and decisions. It fosters a sense of partnership and accountability, encouraging each individual to contribute positively towards the shared vision.\n\nAnother critical aspect of collaboration is the ability to compromise. In any relationship, conflicts and disagreements are inevitable. However, the willingness to find middle ground and make concessions is what differentiates a resilient partnership from a fragile one. Compromise does not imply losing one's identity or values; rather, it involves finding solutions that respect both partners' needs and aspirations.\n\nMoreover, support plays a vital role in collaborative relationships. This encompasses emotional support, such as being present for one another during challenging times, and practical support, which might involve sharing responsibilities or assisting with personal projects. By providing consistent support, partners demonstrate their commitment to each other's well-being and success, reinforcing the collaborative spirit. \n\nTo sustain collaborative efforts, it is essential for partners to periodically reflect on their relationship dynamics. This involves assessing what is working well and

identifying areas that may require improvement. Such reflections can be facilitated through regular check-ins or discussions that focus on the health of the relationship, allowing partners to recalibrate their efforts as needed.
\n\nUltimately, the essence of collaborative efforts in relationships lies in the mutual respect and trust that partners cultivate. By embracing each other's differences and working together towards common goals, individuals can transform their personal issues and struggles into opportunities for growth and connection. This collaborative approach not only enhances the quality of the relationship but also empowers both partners to navigate life's complexities with resilience and grace.

Vision for the Future

The evolving landscape of gender dynamics has led to a growing awareness of the distinct challenges faced by both women and men. As society progresses, it becomes imperative to envision a future where these issues and struggles are not just acknowledged but effectively addressed. The future holds the promise of a more equitable world where gender-based challenges are met with comprehensive solutions and proactive strategies. This vision for the future hinges on the collective efforts of individuals, communities, and institutions to foster an environment of understanding and support.

One of the critical aspects of this future vision is the dismantling of traditional gender roles that have long dictated the societal expectations of women and men. By challenging these outdated norms, society can pave the way for individuals to explore their identities and roles without the constraints of preconceived notions. This shift requires educational reform that integrates gender studies into curriculums from an early age, promoting a culture of inclusivity and respect. Through education, future generations can be equipped with the tools to recognize and challenge gender biases, fostering a society that values equality and diversity.

Technological advancements also play a pivotal role in shaping this future. The digital age provides platforms for voices that were once marginalized, allowing for a broader discourse on gender issues. Social media and online communities have become powerful tools for advocacy and awareness, enabling individuals to share experiences and support one another. As technology continues to evolve, it presents opportunities for innovative solutions to gender-specific challenges, such as virtual support networks and digital mentorship programs. These tools can bridge gaps and provide resources to individuals who might otherwise lack access to support systems.

Moreover, the vision for the future includes a robust legal framework that ensures the protection and empowerment of all genders. This involves implementing policies that promote equal opportunities in the workplace, addressing pay disparities, and combating gender-based violence. Governments and organizations must work collaboratively to create environments where everyone has the opportunity to succeed and thrive without discrimination or bias. Legal reforms must be accompanied by awareness campaigns that highlight the importance of gender equality, encouraging societal shifts in attitudes and behaviors.

In addition to structural changes, the future calls for a cultural transformation that values empathy, understanding, and collaboration. This involves fostering dialogues that encourage individuals to share their experiences and perspectives, promoting mutual respect and solidarity. By cultivating a culture of empathy, society can move towards a more harmonious coexistence where the issues faced by women and the struggles encountered by men are addressed collectively.

Ultimately, this vision for the future is not a distant dream but a tangible goal that requires commitment and action. It is a future where gender is no longer a barrier but a facet of identity that enriches the human experience. Through education, technology, legal reform, and cultural change, the challenges of today can be transformed into the victories of tomorrow. The path to this future is paved with understanding, cooperation, and a shared determination to create a world where everyone has the opportunity to flourish.

ACKNOWLEDGMENTS

This book would not be possible without the care, support and push of:

My wife, First Lady Davantee Smith; thank you for loving me, flaws and all.

My kids (Matheo Jr. Makayla, Matè and Makai) *Yes all the M's lol.*

My parents, Bishop Frederick & Mother Alisa Poitier

My siblings, Clayton and Lynette

My church family. New Bethany Baptist Cathedral - I am honored to be your Pastor.

Overseer Sharon Nairn for the wisdom she instilled in me as it relates to relationships.

My Friend and Publisher, Apostle Paul K. Ellis, Jr. for his friendship, wisdom and help in publishing this book.

Made in the USA
Middletown, DE
07 February 2025